THE HIDDEN FACTOR
Executive Presence

WHAT BUSINESS EXECUTIVES HAVE TO SAY ABOUT
SALLY WILLIAMSON AND
THE HIDDEN FACTOR: EXECUTIVE PRESENCE

"Executive Presence: Often ignored, never defined. Sally's years of expert coaching have enabled her not only to accurately define executive presence, but to show real world ways to build it."

Dan Tarantin
Former President and CEO
Direct General Corporation

"I have personally known Sally for many years. She has an excellent reputation for helping people with their executive presence, particularly with their communication skills. I will always be grateful for the excellent assistance she provided me early in my career."

Mickey Brown
Executive Vice President, Customer Service Organization
Georgia Power Company

"Credibility at the executive level is 100% tied to believability. Through thoughtful coaching, Sally teaches how executive presence can be learned to significantly influence career mobility and key people. She has coached our leaders in executive-level conversations to increase their overall presence, the clarity of their messages and the confidence of the leadership team. Leaders from across the company who participate in Sally's training provide impressive feedback saying, 'Thank you, this was the best personal development I have experienced!'"

CeCe Morken
Vice President and General Manager
Intuit Financial Services

"If your purpose is to influence others in a meaningful and authentic way, Sally Williamson's book will provide invaluable insight. A timely book from an author who personifies *Executive Presence.*"

Jerone Jackson
Co-founder/Principal, The James Paul Group
Former CSO, Miller Heiman

"One of the great things about Sally is she doesn't coach through a megaphone; rather she tailors her training so that it's relevant and impactful and most importantly actionable for her clients."

Lisa Agona
Chief Marketing Officer, Risk Solutions
LexisNexis

"As a trusted resource for our company's development needs, Sally helps us to enhance our high potential team members' attributes that add up to executive presence. She brings a successful roadmap that guides our development programs."

Joe George
Group Vice President, Online Solutions
Manheim, a subsidiary of Atlanta-based Cox Enterprises

"Sally's passion for executive presence has allowed her to build a superb track record in helping business leaders develop effective communication strategies and memorable business presentations. One cannot attend Sally's workshop without walking away prepared to tackle bigger challenges. Sally is an inspiration and always entertaining. You owe it to yourself to read this book!"

Kent Gregoire
Founder and CEO
Responsibility Centered Leadership, Inc.

"Sally worked with members of my department and gave them great confidence and clarity in how they communicate. Her expertise is invaluable in getting professionals ready for their next opportunity."

Carrie Kurlander
Vice President, Communications
Southern Company

"Sally does a great job capturing that certain something that turns ordinary people into extraordinary leaders. Some people are born with that potential power, but it's also a skill that can be coached and developed. Sally helps you understand the charisma of leadership and the chemistry that creates that energy."

Tim Sosbe
Editorial Director
TrainingIndustry.com

"No one does a better job of helping people develop executive presence than Sally Williamson. Her approach is the real deal - authentic, actionable, and spot on."

"I would recommend Sally to anyone. She has given great training and advice to leaders at all levels and I've seen and used Sally's insights and directions to great benefit. From media training to public speaking to executive presence coaching, Sally knows how to take people to their next level."

"I respect Sally's wisdom. Her coaching techniques are valuable for executive leadership skill development. She provides rich insight into the importance of executive presence and how it influences an executive's potential and eventual success. She demonstrates that executive leadership growth requires the delivery of broad messages to influence constituent thinking in order to actively engage them in delivering your vision."

THE HIDDEN FACTOR
Executive Presence
How to Find It, Keep It and Leverage It

SALLY WILLIAMSON

Published by Sally Williamson and Associates, Inc.
Two Buckhead Plaza
3050 Peachtree Road NW, Suite 520
Atlanta, GA 30305

ISBN 978-0-9837069-3-9
Library of Congress Control Number: 2011909368

DEDICATION

To RBL…who filled every room he entered

and

To MHW…who always saves a place for me

Table of Contents

Section 1: What is Presence?

Section 2: How Do You Get Presence?

Section 3: Applying Presence in Today's Business Environment

Appendix

ACKNOWLEDGEMENTS

We owe a heartfelt thank you to our clients who participated in surveys, interviews, phone calls, and a little nagging. While the framework and coaching fundamentals of executive presence belong to Sally Williamson & Associates, the validation of those concepts through our clients' stories and experiences are an invaluable part of the book. I know that your experiences will inspire future leaders to bring a sense of presence to their own careers.

And, I owe a personal thank you to the staff of SW&A. Writing a book while running a company is not an easy feat. In fact, it takes a team. Here's to Stephanie, Lia, and Rhonda who have expanded their roles and commitment for this special project; and, who believe as I do, that executive presence is the hidden factor that becomes the differentiating one.

Section 1:

What is Presence?

1

The Hidden Factor

Conversations about Executive Presence are a lot like the old fairy tale of the emperor with no clothes. Everyone is talking about it, but very few have stepped forward to offer a clear definition of it. It's an elusive idea that keeps creeping into discussions of leadership, executive development, and succession planning.

While many may struggle for the words to define presence, it is very easy to spot in a crowd. Presence fits on a person like a well cut suit. People who have presence fill a room and command attention as if they simply have a right to be there.

For years, people talked about presence as charisma or a God-given trait. Training departments didn't really believe it could be coached or developed in individuals. You were either a born leader or you weren't.

For a while that worked. Leaders floated to the top, and companies found succession to be a pretty easy task as senior managers eased into leadership roles after years of mentoring and observing. But as studies began to talk about baby boomer retirement, it became evident that companies were going to see big gaps in leadership and succession.

As a result, leadership development has become much more proactive. The increased pressure to discover future leaders and to develop managers quickly has created more focus on leadership development programs.

From future leaders to current leaders, companies have built curriculums designed to develop leadership traits. As we've talked to companies about these programs, one topic is consistent in every curriculum: executive presence.

Although I've coached presence for nearly thirty years, the demand for it has intensified recently. The motivation for this book was not only to define presence but also to understand its impact within an organization and across an individual's career. We set out to understand more about the discussions going on inside companies and to see how presence is perceived through a lens other than our own. By marrying executive insights with our coaching expertise, we've been able to define and coach presence and apply these concepts to the current business environment most leaders will face.

We define presence as:

The confidence to express your ideas with conviction and the ability and desire to engage and influence others in the process.

Executive presence is truly a hidden factor because it's hard to capture and yet it's compelling to deliver. Singlehandedly, presence can propel a manager ahead or hold a manager back from success.

This book is for those who are leading today and those who hope to lead tomorrow. May our experience and the input of more than 400 leaders provide the direction you need to develop this hidden factor and to exceed the expectations of any group or audience.

Survey Says

When we began our research we focused on three things:

- Defining presence from an executive's perspective

- Uncovering how executives say they acquire presence

- Aligning our coaching approach with development gaps

Approximately 400 CEOs, C-Level executives, corporate communications executives, and professional development managers completed our survey. We also conducted more than fifty in-depth interviews with Sally Williamson & Associates' senior-level clients to complement it. The results were both confirming and surprising.

The input confirmed that CEOs see presence as an essential part of their job. In fact, 89% of the survey respondents believe that presence helps you get ahead. All of the CEOs interviewed believe that presence is a differentiator. And, 78% of survey respondents said that a lack of presence could hold you back.

What was surprising was the struggle many had to define it and how early in their careers most of these executives began to think about it. You'll hear more about their stories in Chapter 5.

Following is a summary of our key findings.

THE CEO's PERSPECTIVE ON PRESENCE

All of the top executives we surveyed or interviewed valued presence, and all felt they had some aspect of presence, although most continue to work on it. Top executives value presence as an important aspect of doing their job; managers and others around them tend to describe it more as a perception of their ability to do their job.

All believed it was at the core of leadership traits. Throughout the interviews, CEOs were asked about the correlation between leadership and presence. One pointedly said, "You can't be a leader without presence. You might be a CEO, but not a leader."

Another described it as, "Overnight, you go from being a specialist to a generalist. Your messages broaden, your audiences expand, and instantly you have to engage and influence every one of them."

While senior leaders say they convey a sense of presence, they also say they think about presence and try to be intentional about it. Even at the top of their careers they still consider how they need to come across. They work hard to stay focused and deliver an authentic, succinct, and relevant message. In fact, they believe that their ability to do so can calm unsettled issues, inspire unfocused employees, and convince skeptical audiences.

We agree.

HOW PRESENCE IS ACQUIRED

As I mentioned in the first chapter, there has long been a myth that people are either born with presence or they simply don't have it.

We found no evidence in our research or conversations to support this. Only 5% of those surveyed said presence was something they didn't have to think about often. Overwhelmingly, the top executives revealed they think about and work at presence.

So, how did they get presence? They observed it. All the CEOs interviewed said they noticed distinctions and characteristics of leaders early in their career. Most can tell you the moment they knew their sense of presence made a difference in their careers. They were and still are observant, intuitive, and focused on what sets people apart.

In fact, my own conclusion about senior leaders is that many don't realize just how insightful they are. While they mentioned that observation was a critical part in raising their awareness of presence, many of the leaders I know continue to use their observation skills today. They simply notice things that others don't. Their insights have become trusted instincts, and they approach every meeting and interaction with a desire to understand what's going on around them. It sets them apart. And, while that may be a topic for another book altogether, it's evidence that those observation skills are learned early in a career and are still relied upon at the top levels.

Interestingly, as we gather input to prepare for a coaching engagement, I find that C-Suite executives often have the best insights. They may not always define development needs correctly and they might say they don't know how to resolve them. However, their observations about others and their sense of how managers are seen within groups are always spot on. They simply observe a lot.

The second way leaders have said they acquired presence is that they worked hard at it. While many can identify a specific event that launched their careers, they can also cite multiple examples where they thought they would gain visibility and were always ready to put their best foot forward.

No one felt they reached a top leadership role by chance or gained a seat on the management committee by the "luck of the draw." They confirmed that timing had a lot to do with it, but hard work deserved most of the credit. They were prepared and intentional about what they said and how they came across when they said it. They knew that, at some point, it would be their opportunity to shine and they were going to make the most of it. After all, they had observed how it happened time and time again.

Finally, all said that feedback had a lot to do with their awareness of impressions. Many had feedback early in their careers that forced change; others were frustrated that feedback came late. But, all welcomed feedback and saw it as insight and direction to get ahead.

In some of the larger companies, leaders admitted to being intentional about who they wanted to work for in order to gain visibility within a company. They wanted to align their career path with someone who was clearly getting ahead. Others saw high profile projects and knew that the work itself would create an opportunity for exposure.

One executive likened a demanding manager to a football coach. "There was no sugarcoating his feedback. He was tough and he was honest. And while I strongly disliked him at the time, I'm sure his feedback deserves some of the credit for where I am today."

Another said, "As I look back on my career, I am most grateful for the people who invested the time to help me be a better manager. It takes a special mentor to be willing to give someone else's career as much focus as they are trying to give their own. I am, without a doubt, a leader today because someone invested in me."

Collectively, the group said that feedback wasn't always easy to take, but it made all the difference in helping them gain insights early on.

In fact, one leader told me, "Feedback tends to be the indicator of how willing a seasoned manager is to be developed as a leader. When I get resistance to feedback, I simply close the door on that manager's opportunity for advancement."

ALIGNING COACHING FOR RESULTS

Over 65% of those surveyed had also worked with a coach. As we had hoped, our research validated the value coaching can offer to a top executive. While most were aware of presence and observing it, it's not always easy to modify or strengthen impressions just because you want to do so.

Executives confirmed that coaching provides desired feedback in a way that few internal resources can. It can also introduce the right skill sets to help an executive create lasting impressions. As many of our clients confirmed, the ability to present ideas clearly and influence others in the process is more than 75% of what they do every day. You'll read about the skills we coach in Section 2 of the book.

A surprise of the survey was that senior executives buy in to presence and the development of it more than those who are running the development programs. Interestingly, 55% of CEOs said leadership programs can develop presence; only 33% of those in development roles believed this. While working among hundreds of high potential candidates and curriculums, it's been surprising to see that many programs do not provide the fundamental development step of exposure. When asked for the advice they would give managers to understand the "hidden factor" of presence, working with a coach was their second recommendation.

Their first recommendation was observation. Future leaders need an opportunity to observe current leaders. Not only does interaction with top leaders demonstrate presence, it validates the importance of it. We'll talk more about the role of senior leaders in development programs in Chapter 20.

A more complete summary of the survey is in the appendix. The stories and insights of the top executives we interviewed unfold in the following chapters.

3

The Hierarchy of Attributes

O ur research confirmed the same challenge we've seen in many organizations: people define presence differently. While all survey respondents ranked presence high as an attribute, their definitions ranged from physical attire and stature to strategic thinking and influence.

Presence isn't something you give yourself. It's something you earn from those around you who come to respect your right to speak and your ability to lead. Some of our clients call it an "earned authority." It is a combination of behaviors and attitudes that presents a sense of confidence, competence, commitment, and authenticity.

Executive presence is a concept that aligns so closely with leadership that it is often hard to pull them apart. Great leaders have presence and people with presence often make great leaders.

Presence is the balance of personal power and persuasion with compassion and connection.

We took the research input and blended in thirty years of coaching experience to describe presence in a hierarchy of attributes. The hierarchy encompasses the range of definitions for presence we heard and explains why these definitions may seem vague but are really just broad.

Considering presence as a range of skills instead of a single narrow one has helped development managers think about how to develop it in future leaders. It also helps leaders understand that these attributes develop over time and expand as their role in the company expands. What is expected of a senior leader is simply more demanding than what is expected of a middle manager.

Below are the concepts that support the visual on the opposite page:

Level I: Physical. These attributes incorporate the physical look of an individual including their refinement, polish, and appearance.

Level II: Functional. These attributes include both learned skills and personality traits and describe how we observe someone doing their job.

All of the people surveyed, from communication and development managers to CEOs, agreed that it took Level I and Level II attributes to get beyond a mid-manager role. But, those in senior level positions saw executive presence as more of a term of engagement.

Level III: Rational. These attributes dive into traits necessary to engage others and range from persuading and influencing

EXECUTIVE PRESENCE HIERARCHY OF ATTRIBUTES

EMOTIONAL
- Authentic
- Believable
- Charismatic
- Confident
- Empathetic
- Intuitive
- Transparent

RATIONAL
- Accepts feedback/criticism
- Commands a room
- Collaborative
- Credible
- Engaging
- Good listener
- Influential
- Persuasive
- Strong communicator
- Strategic-thinking

FUNCTIONAL
- Detail-focused
- Driven
- Expertise
- Initiative
- Outspoken
- Preparedness
- Professionalism
- Traditional-thinking

PHYSICAL
- Attire
- Physical presence
- Refined/Polished

Differentiation

Cost of Entry

to listening. This is where leaders begin to differentiate themselves and often move ahead of one another at the C-Level.

Level IV: Emotional. Once executives shift their focus off of themselves and onto their listeners, their ability to engage opens them up to connect at a very personal and believable level. The highest attributes tied to executive presence are empathy, authenticity, and transparency.

While my experience is that people use words all over the spectrum to define executive presence, there were a few notable trends.

When people are asked to describe a person they believe has presence, they start with words in the lower part of the hierarchy. Most will say someone who comes across as professional, intentional, really owns their space, and looks as if they have a right to be here.

But when you ask more about how they respond to the person with presence, people begin to describe how they feel about them rather than how they visually see them. This leads to words like persuasive, engaging, interesting, and authentic.

The more removed an individual is from a top executive, the more likely they are to describe the physical and functional traits. They haven't really experienced anything else. But, as people have more interaction with those they are describing, they become more critical of the "influencing" traits and presence becomes more important in how an executive or manager impacts others.

Interestingly, as executives rated themselves, those who were focused on the emotional attributes described at the top of the hierarchy were the more effective leaders that we interviewed.

All of the skills outlined in the hierarchy are coachable. I've been a part of making it work in many companies. Through the years I've learned that when companies and future leaders understand the significance and impact of presence, the coaching process can help a leader shift from the more physical and functional attributes to the more rational and emotional connections.

It certainly did in the stories you're about to read.

4

Alignment with Leadership

The impact of presence played out before me several years ago. I happened to be with a group of senior leaders who were together for a few days of planning meetings. Their CEO, John, had announced his retirement and the Board had just announced his replacement, Stephen. The Board felt the meeting provided a nice opportunity for the leadership team to meet Stephen over dinner.

Including other managers at the meeting, 150 people attended the dinner event. As we were seated, John, the retiring CEO, came in with a small group and headed to a table to sit down. Nothing happened for fifteen to twenty minutes and the caterer began to serve dinner. The vice president of communications happened to be at our table and worried something had gone wrong so he went over to John's table to ask if Stephen was no longer coming. He returned with a disheartened look on his face. It turned out the new CEO was part of the small group that came in with John. He was at the table; he just went unnoticed. He missed an important opportunity to own the room.

Matters got worse as John stood up to introduce Stephen. The new CEO had no presence and the crowd was able to form an immediate comparison. Although the new CEO didn't linger with the team for the remaining planning days, his impression sure did. And it was not a strong one. The leadership team lacked confidence in him and had already begun to doubt his ability to lead the company.

Since I was involved with this team, I saw this scenario play out over a number of months. The communications group was charged with "promoting" Stephen and tried to help him build credibility outside the company through industry meetings, keynote speeches, and high visibility boards. The thought was that if he gained respect and visibility outside the company, he could overcome the poor impressions that had formed inside the company. Well over $500,000 was invested in this effort.

I met with Stephen once to talk through the benefits of coaching. He was interested in improving his image; he just didn't think the timing was right. And sadly, it never was. After twelve months the Board decided his lack of presence was too big of a hurdle to overcome. They began a new search with presence as one of their top criteria.

A conversation with a lead partner in a search firm confirmed that my story is not uncommon. "In an executive search you line up competencies," she said. "And while we often don't talk about it, in the end it will be the hidden factor, the presence factor, that wins. If you don't have it, you won't get the job."

A female executive shared a similar story of working in a company where the CEO was more of a figurehead. He didn't have a lot of presence and didn't like to be the center of attention. He made the mistake of passing the communicator's role and the leadership role to the number two man in the company. At the time this occurred they worked in tandem to lead the company. It was commonplace to hear that Mr. Jones was the CEO, but Mr. Chandler ran the company. Eventually that led to an early retirement for Mr. Jones.

One of our objectives for the interviews and surveys we conducted was to identify stories and examples that would validate the impact of presence. Consistently, we found the attributes of presence were very similar to the attributes of leadership.

That's why the concept of presence should be included and coached in every leadership development program.

Historically, development groups have been reluctant to include skills or competencies they felt were out of an individual's control. After all, if presence is defined by the impressions of others, can you really impact what others say and feel toward you? I believe you can, and that it's critical for future leaders to begin thinking about these impressions early on in their careers.

What would happen if every leadership program talked to managers about the attributes of presence? You would find that raising awareness of presence helps managers understand the expectations of future listeners and the essential skills it takes to influence others to work hard, rather than just working harder yourself. You can't control every impression or reaction around you, but you can make choices that impact many of them.

One executive said, "If I'd realized how much of leadership was about influencing and motivating others, I would have paid more attention to how my mentors did it. Success for me has come more from understanding the needs of those around me than really thinking of my own needs and efforts."

Another executive said, "You will never fully control any situation as a leader. You can learn every management skill backwards and forwards, but in a critical business situation you're more impacted by the skills of those on your team than by your own. And that's why it's imperative to establish a presence with a team that allows you to have the trust and respect you'll need to lead the team through a tough situation."

A third executive summed it up this way, "Presence and communication rank #1 and #2 under leadership traits. They are closely wound together, although not the same thing. You can surround yourself with brilliant people, but you can't use someone else to portray a sense of presence. That's yours alone as a leader to portray."

The leaders we interviewed value presence, and they understand the need and desire to engage their audiences. You will find their thoughts interesting as the next chapter summarizes how they got presence, how they use it today, and their advice for helping others gain it.

5

Impressions from the C-Suite

When a coaching engagement begins, I usually frame up the process and ask an executive if he or she has specific questions about the impact of coaching.

One of the most common questions is: Can presence really be coached? The answer is unequivocally, **yes**! Not every trait you observe about someone will fit on someone else in exactly the same way. There is no cookie cutter approach to presence. But you can learn to exude confidence, to engage an audience, and to gain a level of commitment behind your message. Presence looks different on different people.

Our C-Suite executives defined presence as:

- Compelling
- Intuitive
- Poise
- Gravitas
- You know it the minute it enters a room

- Inspirational
- Intentional
- Integrity
- It's clarity of intention

When asked if they believed their own presence was innate, only 2 out of 400 said yes. Instead, most leaders said presence was intentional. They thought about it and worked hard to achieve it.

One CEO said, "It's the feeling of being 'on.' When I walk into a room or step onto a stage, presence is a huge part of grabbing an audience's attention. Without it anything you say has far less interest."

Another said, "I think of it as a conscious competence. I'm aware of it and aware of working at it."

Other comments include:

"Presence isn't a part of my natural personality. I learned it through coaching. I kick myself sometimes for not handling things well. I'm still a work in progress."

"I'm painfully aware when I'm not the leader I need to be. Hopefully, that's less likely to happen these days."

"I think about it [presence] more as my career has advanced. Intuitively, I know about it. But, I'm more intentional about it now. I review my calendar every night and think about clarity in meetings and defining what people need to take away."

Collectively, today's leaders say that awareness is a key factor in gaining presence. It may surprise you to know that all of the leaders we interviewed and surveyed were aware of presence early on in their careers. For some, awareness happened in childhood. From athletes to ballerinas, school thespians to class officers, many of our respondents sought leadership early in life. But not all of them were so inclined. Some were shy. Others were introverted or intellectual. However, at some point, they all began to pay attention.

Excerpts from their experiences:

"I worked for someone who had presence. I thought it was very powerful. I was intrigued at how often people sought his advice and worked to gain his respect. I wanted to be like that."

"I was handed a significant presentation to a key customer early in my career. My boss said, 'I know you can do this,' and I learned that I could do it and handle the pressure. From that point, I knew that communication skills would be critical to my success."

"I was one of five African Americans in the practice group of a consulting firm. An African American partner began to mentor us and told us that we needed to make something happen when we walked into a room. He said, 'Get yourself noticed like she does,' and he pointed to me. He said, 'You have that quality.'"

All agreed they became aware of presence by observing the behaviors and attitudes around them and the attributes that elicited a response. Feedback was a critical part of every leader's development.

"Best coaching advice I got was, 'If you want a position, act like you're in the position.'"

"Early on, a boss told me I was too defensive. He told me to let people disagree with me. Hear them out. They might add value."

"I had a manager who took out a piece of paper and drew a line down the middle. He developed a column for pros and a column for cons. After any presentation or meeting, he had a sheet full of feedback in each column. It doesn't take long to catch on when feedback is that direct."

"Even as a young CEO, I got feedback. A board member would pull me aside and say, 'If you'd said it like this, you could have gotten your way.'"

"Communication wasn't a natural strength for me. Thank heavens I had a boss who told me so. In fact, he said I was awful. He said, 'You may think you delivered information, but we never got your message.' That changed my thinking about communication and how people responded to me."

Some of our interviewees hold the senior communications role within their companies. While they shared insights on their own skills, they also have responsibility for evaluating their peers and leveraging the more effective communicators to position the company brand. Their insights were revealing.

"I see presence or the lack of it every time I sit in a meeting with my peers. One member of our leadership team brought up an idea recently that just felt redundant to the group. No one wanted to hear about it again but he insisted on barreling through his ideas. You could see the lack of respect echoed on the faces around the table. It will take him a long time to recover from that."

"Some of our top leaders are more comfortable in their skin than others but they all know how to turn on presence when they need to. I work with one executive who doesn't have it, and I give him about six months before he loses the opportunity."

Whether feedback came early or at a midpoint in their career, all of these leaders welcomed it and tried to adjust to it.

When asked for advice on how to gain presence, they recommend the same approach to those who are coming behind them.

"If you wait for the company to come and tap you for development, you may have to wait awhile. Seek feedback and absorb it."

"No one on my leadership team takes presence as seriously as I do. And that's because they don't see the impact of it from the CEO's seat yet. But I'd be willing to bet that the person who begins to exude more of it will be the one you see in my role some day."

"Get help early. I don't want to follow someone who is trying to get it; I want to follow a leader who already has it."

"The best way to gain presence is to learn a formula for it and then work hard to adopt pieces of it and make it your own. The hardest work comes after the coaching when you have to integrate it into everything you do."

"Presence is the hardest thing to coach in our organization. It takes time to build impressions. You can't just wake up one morning and expect people to see you differently. Start working on it now."

"A great time for coaching is as you transition from a contributor to an influencer."

While the leaders' thoughts validate the importance of presence, they also validate the invisible roadblock that a lack of presence creates.

For a summary of the executive input, see the appendix at the end of the book.

6

The Invisible Roadblock

For every executive we've coached who took the initiative to gain presence, there are two more who've been sent to us because they hit the invisible roadblock. That doesn't mean there are more people who lack presence than people who have it. That means managers and new executives wait too late to get help, so coaching becomes focused on removing roadblocks or changing impressions.

In our interviews we asked for examples of people who got ahead with presence and those who were held back without it. As you might imagine, there were far more who missed the chance than those who actually moved ahead to senior leadership. According to the interviewed executives, here's why:

"Middle management is the ceiling point without presence. You'll watch more engaged managers pass you by. Beyond middle management, you have to have the ability to influence and lead people."

"Your company may compete outside of your doors with others in the industry; but you personally are competing inside the doors with those who are sitting around you."

"It just takes so much longer if advancement is based only on merit because people have to be willing to take the time to see your talents."

"Within every company there are internal powers or informal leaders. Presence has a huge impact on this. I have seen many who were passed over because they lacked presence. Often, it's someone who has the time and experience in the company and by many accounts 'deserved' the top position. But they simply couldn't frame up their ideas clearly. They just couldn't get a group to follow."

"At some point success becomes how much you can get done through others. The lack of presence can become a true roadblock when you are measured more by your ability to drive others to results rather than gaining results yourself."

Most of those completing our survey were top leaders who are involved in selecting the next leaders rather than identifying those who have potential to lead down the road. So it stands to reason that if they're holding someone back, it's because they feel it's too late to work on impressions. There's just not time to develop this powerful tool as you step up to bat.

My experience is that presence can be established within an organization over several different scenarios and over an extended period of time. Our interviews with senior leaders back up this theory. But there were several stories that suggested executives felt they had a defining moment in their careers where they knew it was their time to shine.

The common themes to their stories are preparation, participation, and a little risk.

"I was a senior manager running an important department when we had a contract dispute with customers. It led to a series of lawsuits and as a company we were focused on holding our position rather than resolving the problem. The more I sat in meetings and talked to customers, the more I realized that our customers' position on our contracts was right and we were wrong. I drafted a controversial white paper to the CEO recommending that we back down. It was a risky proposition suggesting that we base our relationships on trust and customer loyalty rather than pricing. I sold my idea to the CEO and the Board and my career skyrocketed from there."

"I was a senior manager at the time our company was purchased. Our division was to be part of an analyst call to announce the acquisition and talk through the integration. The president of our division was going on vacation so he said that I should represent the division. I practiced my key points and delivered them with confidence. Afterwards, the CEO of the company who acquired us congratulated all of the speakers on a successful launch. He felt the analysts believed our message and our strategy. Then, he mentioned me by name and said he wished everyone had my confidence. Within four months of this acquisition I was already on the radar of the new company's CEO."

"I participated in a leadership program and took the simulations seriously. In our final exercise we had to prepare a presentation and recommendation to our leadership team. I did my homework and was ready to ask thought provoking questions to kickoff the presentation. The leadership team took note and after the program ended I was invited to sit in on senior meetings. I immediately noticed that no one wanted to speak up so I began to do so. I asked lots of questions and tactfully challenged things that didn't seem right. It became more the norm rather than the exception to include me in key discussions. And before long, I had a seat at the table."

"I was an attorney in our legal department so I was involved in transactional meetings for our company. In preparation for meetings, I prepared way beyond my area of expertise to try and expand my role and my contribution. I was three levels below anyone else in the room and yet I was often the most informed on the topic and situation. The team took notice. I was prepared and knowledgeable. I earned my seat and voice at the table."

Do you hear the common themes in these stories?

All of these leaders put in the time and preparation to participate. And, when they did, their sense of presence and confidence was noticed and they set a lasting impression.

For each of these success stories there are five more that speak of missed opportunities. In every coaching engagement I hear the good, the bad, and the ugly.

"I have been a senior manager for four years. My boss began talking about an upcoming manager's retreat and my opportunity to present our plans for a new initiative in the coming year. I was slated to make the presentation and he told me that I really needed to work on my delivery skills so that I would put my best foot forward. I never took the time to do that, and I did a poor job of presenting a great idea. I realized my mistake when I looked out at the senior management team that day. After the presentation I told my boss that I should have worked harder and I wanted another chance before the senior team. He just looked at me and said, 'I think it will be awhile. It would be a mistake to put you in front of the group until they've had time to forget what they saw today.' That was two years ago, and I haven't presented to the senior leaders since."

"I participated in a high potential program within our company two years ago. I didn't take the program seriously and probably didn't take advantage of the opportunities for exposure to the senior leaders of the company. But there were three people in my group who seemed to make it a priority. I noticed that they were always willing to lead discussions and report in on projects with senior leaders. Ironically, I read about their promotions eighteen months later."

Presence isn't just about getting noticed, but it does make a difference in whether people begin to pay attention to you and take note of your capabilities. It's an essential ingredient to leadership and influence, and it's one that takes some time to acquire.

One of our clients said it best:

"In our company I've seen people adopt aggressive skills to fight for the top seat only to find that it takes humility and patience to be a CEO. If results were enough, everyone would be CEO."

So, how do you get presence? Our next section highlights the coachable skills we use to help both managers and executives gain the confidence and conviction to express their ideas in a way that engages and influences others.

Section 2:

How Do You Get Presence?

7

The "Coachability" Factor

I n Chapter 2, I said that one of the goals of our research was to align our coaching approach with development gaps. The survey confirmed that we are coaching to the attributes described as presence in our research.

But the survey also confirmed that skepticism exists within development programs about how much presence can really be coached. I call it the "coachability" factor. From my own experience I've learned that this skepticism comes because most people who run executive development programs have heard so many different explanations and definitions of presence that they know this can't possibly be a "one size fits all" skill.

They're right. But, presence is coachable. Rather than trying to define it broadly, my position has been that it should be seen as a spectrum of skills just like leadership. What matters most is being able to define a starting point for an executive or manager and identifying the steps it will take to help him or her move toward presence. See the Hierarchy of Attributes on page 17.

At the start of any coaching relationship, we gather input and feedback from communications or development teams who have recommended coaching. We see 360° evaluations, videotapes, peer assessments, and personality tests. In fact, we get inundated with data, and it's helpful in understanding perceptions and impressions.

But, to me, the most important step of coaching is awareness. What I really want to know at the start of an engagement is not only what an executive or manager has been told (i.e. the feedback and evaluation tools) but more importantly, what he or she has heard. There is usually a significant difference in the two.

Too often the people giving feedback try to solve the gap at the same time they point it out. So most people I see come not only with feedback but also with someone's recommendation of how they solve their communication issue. As you might imagine, those recommendations are remembered more than the feedback itself. That's why I see many people trying to do the wrong thing with the best of intentions.

For example, take a young manager who operates at top speed. He has a lot of energy and in customer meetings he rushes through things. He talks fast, he interrupts the customer to share ideas, and he squirms in his seat while he's listening. The sales director gives him this feedback and tells him that he has to slow down. To help him the director "recommends" he should try counting to five before he says anything. (This is an ill-advised technique for pausing.) With the best of intentions, the director may have made matters worse because the manager is still rushing, he still interrupts, and he still squirms. But now, we can see him thinking about something else before he speaks.

This is a classic example of giving recommendations with feedback. The feedback is good; it identifies many of the distractors that the director experienced. The recommendation is not good. Instead, our coaching would be to get the young manager to settle, slow down, and focus on listening to the customer. Listening is really the key to help the manager understand why his style isn't working.

Presence coaching is difficult. It requires a clear understanding of where the current perceptions and impressions originated. Actually, the coaching candidate doesn't have to agree with the feedback or assessment. He only has to accept the impressions or perceptions that led to the feedback.

Once there is buy-in to those impressions, we can chart a course for what it will take to change them or strengthen them.

We work from a coaching process that includes three core steps:

- Assessment & Awareness

- Core Skill Development

- Situational Support

Section 2 of the book highlights each of these components and offers ways to work on your own presence or to help develop it in others.

The coachability factor is driven by desire. If an individual understands the impressions that his actions are creating and values the benefit of trying to adjust those impressions, then the coachability factor is quite high.

Through the eyes of a CEO, "The day I stop listening to feed-back will be the day I make my biggest mistake."

8

Linking Presence & Communication

As we head into our coaching concepts it's worth noting that communication skills are the basis for building the core skills of presence. The reason is the attributes of presence are most noticed and noted when someone is in a speaking or communicating role.

If you read through the memorable moment stories in Chapter 6, you noticed they were tied to key presentations or communication situations. This is a tough pill to swallow for many executives.

I often hear:

"It's so frustrating to think that a fifteen-minute presentation really weighs stronger on the Board's mind than my presence in those meetings for the last six months."

"This group knows me. How can my presence on my feet be so important? "

"I have a great relationship with the CMO. I'm shocked that she feels I'm not confident enough to pitch our strategy to the leadership team next week."

Frustrating? Maybe it is. But is it real? Yes, very much so.

The need for communication skills intensifies as you climb the corporate ladder. When I coach a CEO on a presentation and I sense that he isn't focused on it, I ask how significant he feels the message is. The response is usually, "This presentation isn't that big of a deal. It's just to kick-off the year with employees." Then I ask, "So after this meeting, when will you pull all your employees together again for an update?" Typically the reaction is, "I'll do a mid-year update in six months." My response is, "So your 'not so important message' is going to live with the employee group for six months. Can you think of anything else you're working on right now that has that kind of impact?"

That usually gets their attention.

It's easier to communicate as a mid-level manager. While your skills may not be as good as they should be, you can re-pair impressions in a few days if you interact with the group frequently.

But as a senior leader that's just not the case. If employees only see you two or three times a year, impressions are more weighted and they last much longer. Imagine an external audience. If I hear you speak at an industry event or on an analyst call my only impression of you is based on those ten to fifteen minutes.

There are different ways to address some of the attributes of presence. For us, helping an executive strengthen his impressions in front of his core audiences is the best starting place.

The CEOs we interviewed agree. One said, "When you step up to the podium, you step into a testing zone. You validate or negate your ability to be a leader."

9

Assessment & Awareness

I talked about awareness as the basis of coachability in Chapter 7. Let me offer a little more insight on how we get there.

I said that what matters more to me than having feedback and impressions about an executive is to understand what he or she actually took away from an evaluation or assessment. It's hard to hear "you need more presence," and not everyone does hear it. Defining a starting point for coaching requires a good awareness of what an individual hopes to change or strengthen.

Our coaching process begins with understanding an executive's environment and key audiences. I ask about key relationships at work and can usually figure out which ones are difficult and which ones are comfortable. This helps me tie situational exercises to key events later in the coaching process.

While coaching will be an intense look at your skills, it will be an even more intense look at your listeners. Ultimately, if you can understand what people expect from you and then de-

47

liver on it, you'll be effective. Great communication is not totally about you as the speaker, it's much more about the listener.

Most resistance to coaching comes from a lack of awareness. While I have often worked with someone who was less than thrilled about the idea of coaching, I can usually establish buy-in by raising awareness of impressions and framing the perception of their audiences.

This may be one of the advantages of an outside resource or coach. My input and assessment is very objective. I've never seen this individual before and certainly don't have any skin in the game or need to be anything less than honest. If an individual doesn't buy into an assessment or evaluation, I rarely argue with them. I offer my assessment of them that day and use it as a modified starting point. Eventually, when they settle into the coaching process, we will get back to the feedback from their work environment. My job is really to interpret the feedback rather than reinforce it.

Often I get an "aha" moment with a client when I begin to ask questions about impact and takeaways. Many executives don't think about what others are supposed to do with their messages or what kind of response they're really driving. When I discuss impact, most executives talk about themselves in terms of pushing out information. They rarely think about pulling in a group of listeners. Therefore, this establishes a good foundation for understanding what presence really is.

We establish impact with a few key benchmarks. In the first seven seconds, any listener can establish up to eleven impressions of you.

Those impressions are based on: physical posture, the sound of your voice, the words themselves. Those three components add up to 100%, but the breakdown is surprising:

55% - physical posture

38% - the sound of your voice

7% - words alone

Overall, coaching is about raising the awareness of impact in these key areas and then changing habits. The impressions of presence come from deliberate and/or unintentional habits. Once we lay a framework for coaching and have buy-in to the general direction, we're ready to work on core skills.

10

Coachable Skill - Physical Posture

There is no doubt that the use of the body creates a significant impression. In fact, it's 55% of our total first impression of a person. But posture is more than how you stand and how you look. It's an awareness of how you use your body, and ultimately using it in a settled and open way that conveys a sense of confidence and credibility.

People who define presence as "you can just tell when someone enters a room," "they really own the room," or "they seem comfortable in their own skin" are responding to the physicalness of presence.

The Purely Visual

The truth is a portion of presence is purely visual. Some people consider visual image to be the superficial part. But people notice how you put yourself together.

Visual image has gotten a little complicated with casual work environments, but, ironically, the more relaxed the environment, the more the leaders stand out. People with presence are deliberate about how they look and what they wear.

My coaching advice for you is to be intentional. When you get dressed in the morning for an important meeting or event, be sure that what people see is exactly the image or impression you want to make. Among all the coaching steps and techniques around presence, visual image is the easiest adjustment to make.

Yet, one out of every ten coaching engagements we take on has a visual image element. It's surprising to me that people don't take it seriously. But this is an area of awareness and feedback that is seldom addressed. If you don't explore this for yourself, it is not likely that anyone will help you with it. Visual image feedback ranks high on the list of things managers and executives avoid in feedback sessions.

One executive told me recently that she stepped in to offer visual image feedback to a young woman who was skipped over for promotion. Senior managers felt she wasn't taken seriously and didn't come across as knowledgeable. The truth was they didn't feel she made a good first impression. When the executive gave her the feedback the woman said, "I can't believe I've been with this company for ten years and no one has ever told me to change the way I dress."

We could all use an evaluation of how we present ourselves. Consider it your visual image check-up. Even with clients who dress well, I recommend having two or three "great image looks" that you know work well and you can rely on for the big moments.

The Power of the Body

If you think about presence as really owning your space, you'll quickly see that people aren't created equal. A man who is 6'4" standing next to a woman who is 5'4" may seem to have more physical presence because he simply takes up more space.

But this doesn't mean he ultimately has more presence. Physical presence involves settling and opening the body so that the listener's impression is you are confident and interested in involving them in your topic. Our 6'4" man may trade off his presence by slouching his shoulders or closing his body. Likewise, the 5'4" woman can hold her own beside him by opening her body and arms to extend her space.

People who really own their space exude confidence through a settled stance. In our coaching we work on physical stance and overall use of the body to raise awareness of how to own your space and get the body forward to a listener.

Settled vs. Pumped - Relaxed vs. Tight

It seems simple but it isn't always. Many people find it hard to focus on how their body feels and what it's doing. Instead, they focus their attention in their heads as they think through messages and carefully choose their words. For most people, it takes deliberate intention to get settled and grounded on their feet.

As I look at posture and body stance, I often find that people carry stress across their shoulders. Try telling an executive who's carrying the weight of the world and his fourth quarter

53

earnings on his shoulders that he needs to relax. It's just not as easy as it should be.

A few years ago, I worked with an executive who was so physically tight he experienced lower back pain. On a video I saw a difference in the height of his shoulders. He kept telling me he was relaxed, but I knew differently. His shoulders were so tight that when I touched them he cringed. I used several techniques to help him drop his shoulders and showed him the difference on video. Once he saw and felt the difference, he was willing to work on it. Ultimately he reduced his lower back pain as well.

A lot about gaining presence in front of a group makes us feel as if we should be pumped up, ready to bring great energy and effort to a situation. While you want to convey commitment, the physical rush of adrenaline can cause tightness in the body. One of my first lessons to an executive is helping him or her understand how relaxed the body should be and what it will take to get it there.

For some, it means work outside of coaching. I've referred people to yoga, massage, and other means to raise awareness of a settled body and to help people feel more in control of body choices.

In an Executive World

Once we set goals for new body choices, I coach the executive through key situations to make sure the new skills are applied. Posture and body choices are easy to understand, but changing habits can be hard.

Here are some of the more common situations and suggestions for establishing a strong physical presence:

Large Audiences: Most executives deal with large audiences and big stages. In a coaching relationship, I work to understand how someone best fits within a space and takes advantage of it. This is not the same for everyone. Shorter people do better toward the front of a stage and away from lecterns. An executive who moves around a lot needs to learn how to bring his energy forward and use movement deliberately.

Over the years we've seen many poor choices create bad impressions. Microphones and teleprompters set at the wrong height can cause a slouching posture. Spotlights defining small spaces can narrow physical space and create closed postures.

If you spend any time on a big stage, you need to learn how to make that space work for you rather than trying to work within the space.

Beginnings: I spend more time working on settled posture at the beginning of a meeting or presentation than at any other point. This is because learning to be intentional about beginnings is a great way to establish presence. You set your pace at this point in communication and the more deliberate the pace, the more settled the individual. When I'm rehearsing a big event with an executive, we don't just practice the opening. We practice the walk to the stage, the placement of notes, etc. All of these movements are part of initial impressions.

Comfort Zones: Although most of my coaching time is spent on things that don't work well for an executive, I always like to understand someone's comfort zone. Style and presence should be consistent across all types of situations, but they aren't for most people. By understanding what works in someone's comfort zone, I can help apply strengths to other situations.

Interviews: A lot of our clients work with us on interviews with media, analysts, employees, etc. For most people, the Q&A component is one of the toughest because they feel less in control of the content and direction of the discussion. Over the years I've noticed this is a situation where bad posture habits are most prevalent. Learning to open the body and come forward makes all the difference in establishing physical presence in these situations.

It is a natural reflex to pull back from a tough question. Watch any news show and notice how interviewees physically respond to questions. Their posture usually gives away discomfort with a topic long before their content does. By learning to come forward or lean into tough questions, executives physically "own" the question, the space, and the moment.

Coaching Others on Physical Posture

I'm often asked to provide tips on coaching others. Within any corporation or business there are communications and development people who find themselves in a position to offer feedback or advice for improving presence.

I tell my clients the biggest challenge with helping others is moving beyond feedback. As I mentioned in Chapter 7, I often work with people who have been given bad coaching advice. Unless you've had experience in really changing behaviors or physical posture, stick to feedback on things you actually see rather than making assumptions about what you think may be causing the problem.

For example, your CEO is rehearsing for a shareholder meeting. In the first run-through he appears to be in constant motion; he's shifting his weight side to side and swirling his arms around. When he asks for feedback you should tell him that he appears unsettled and is moving around a lot. However, many would offer a perceived solution by telling him to "stop using your hands" or "stop moving your feet." The truth is he needs to slow down. His rate of speech is driving both the movement of his feet and his hands. If he simply locks his hands or his feet, the nervous energy will shift to something else. Until you know what is actually causing a problem, you're always better to stick to your impressions of what you actually see.

Videotaping is a great coaching technique for posture. It's easy to see the use of the body. Even if you haven't been asked to give feedback, I recommend taping corporate meetings, presentations, etc., which creates an automatic feedback tool for executives. Some physical issues are easily understood and adjusted by executives themselves if they only see what their audience is seeing.

11

Coachable Skill - Commitment & Involvement

O nce past physical posture, most of the attributes people describe about presence relate to an executive's ability to motivate and involve a group. Energy, effort, involvement, and urgency make a group want to sit up and listen. Speakers who are described as charismatic, entertaining, and interesting all have the ability to get behind their words and make others feel as if it matters to them that you, as a listener, buy into what they're saying.

While the sound of the voice was only 38% of the first impression and less than the visual impact of the body, the voice is the more powerful of the communication tools. Here's why. Our work on the body is about getting people relaxed, open, and settled as communicators. The voice is about getting the speaker behind his or her words and involved in getting a point across. Learning to use your voice effectively is one of the most important core skills of presence.

Is the Person I Heard, the Same Person I See?

Communication directors are often surprised to find that the commitment and interest an executive can build in a room seems to vanish when they put him on a conference call. The energy level drops and the executive can seem uninterested and flat to the listener. This is a sure sign the physical presence was carrying more of the impression than the communications group may have realized.

The input I usually get is, "He's just not comfortable with this size group," or "She says she can't speak without a live audience." We're all moving too fast these days for an executive to be wedded to only a few speaking mediums. (See Chapter 17) For many, it takes a shift in perspective to understand where energy really comes from and how to use the voice for impact.

Most of our coaching takes place in our conference room. I will always remember one executive who came in for his first session and told me the room was too small for him. "I'm a really dynamic speaker and I like to dominate a room. I need more space to move so that you can see the impact of my energy."

While our conference room is not a grand ballroom, it easily holds twenty to thirty people. So I was surprised at the feedback and eager to see how this "dynamic speaker" would use the space. As he began it was as if someone had literally wound him up and pushed him to center stage. He paced back and forth and flung his arms up every few steps. I was so busy watching him that I had no idea what he actually said. When we viewed a videotape of him I asked him to be a member of his own audience and think about what real impact he, the speaker, would have on the listener.

He said he felt flat in his delivery and uninvolved in the topic. His thought was that he should move more and work harder. He did need to work harder, but with his mouth and not his feet. His idea of energy and commitment was wound up in movement and wasn't accomplishing anything for the listener.

We coach executives to get their energy forward and their intent behind their words. What they quickly learn is that commitment comes from the voice, not the body.

Speaking with Your Whole Face

One of the most critical coaching steps with voice is learning to use the whole face when you speak. If you watch someone who has low energy or a monotone voice, you'll notice they don't open their mouth much when they speak. Opening the mouth and articulating clearly is imperative to building energy behind words, but it also brings expression to the face. When we listen, we take in someone's whole face. If it lacks expression, it's very difficult to buy into the message or to feel as if the speaker really cares about our reaction.

Ultimately, having commitment takes effort. The person working harder to get behind the words is more expressive and more interesting to watch.

You can easily test this impact for yourself. Stand in front of a mirror and say a simple sentence, "I need the report at two o'clock," in a very monotone voice. As you watch, you'll see the mouth doesn't move much. Now, repeat the sentence and say it like you really mean it. Notice how the whole face engages as you bring expression through your eyes, mouth, and brows.

The Power of the Voice

Commitment and involvement are the most common skills we work on with managers who are newly promoted to executive roles. The reason is the voice doesn't always get used to its full capacity. An executive who was comfortable and effective talking to audiences of 50-100 people, may seem very low on energy and interest when he faces a crowd of 500.

While physical presence is easily transferable, the concepts of commitment and engagement are not as easy to transition as groups get larger. Most executives need to know how to project the voice forward and to the back of a room. This isn't often tested at a manager's level.

Projection is the skill that makes someone effective with remote audiences and conference calls. If you have energy and commitment in your voice, your ability to send it forward and project it makes all the difference to a listener whose only impression is the voice. Many of my exercises draw chuckles as executives find that coaching often includes reading children's books or crazy rhymes and quotes but it's all designed to raise awareness of the voice choices and to show the impact of voice.

Through the years, I've worked with many soft-spoken or monotone executives. I've learned that changing the quality of the voice can feel daunting and overwhelming. So I ask them to spend only five minutes every day thinking about the exercises I've given them and applying them to a phone call. My goal is to raise awareness of how it feels to work harder, so they will recognize what it takes and begin to do it more routinely.

I also create early morning exercises for busy executives. A common one is changing their voicemail by 7:30am. I'll call and listen to the message and leave feedback on how they sound. Then, at some point during the day, they return the call and leave a message trying to correct the issues I've identified. Again, this raises awareness and gets an individual thinking about effort.

Energy in the voice is all about working harder to get your point across. Voice coaching is more difficult because we hear it rather than view it. But I've seen hundreds of executives improve their impact by simply focusing on their ability to get behind the words and on sending their energy forward to the group.

The Power of Silence

It's ironic to mention silence in the voice chapter as one of the more impactful tools. But, it's true.

Senior executives are easy to spot by how they enter a room and it has a lot to do with pace. It's deliberate and intentional. Pause helps an executive keep that sense of deliberateness and intention in communication.

In fact, we coach many executives to use pause deliberately at the start of any communication. It's a powerful way to engage a group and establish a sense of presence from the very beginning. Pause says I'm in charge and setting the pace and direction of communication. When people rush into their remarks they throw away this moment of ownership and usually cannot recapture it.

I worked with one female executive who was a roadrunner. Everything about her and the way she worked was fast-paced. This created great impressions when she was a manager because people believed she could get a lot done and move things along. But, once she was considered for a more senior role, those impressions shifted. The feedback I received before meeting her was, "She just seems too flighty for the role. We are worried that she doesn't spend enough time thinking through her actions, and we're afraid she may be more of a busy bee than a thoughtful executive."

I met her for the first time by going to a rehearsal for a presentation she was giving the following week. She entered the room like a whirling dervish with lots of energy, moving fast, and totally unaware of how that was perceived. She asked for my feedback after the first run-through, and I told her I only wanted to work on one thing before the presentation. She was surprised that we spent an hour on how she walked to the stage and settled before the group. I didn't touch her content at this point or practice the full presentation again. It was only about pace, and it made a tremendous difference.

The CEO called after the presentation and told me he was pleased at how much more thoughtful her message was than when he'd heard it the previous week. The message hadn't changed; it was all about her pace and the use of pause.

Pause can also create a good connection between the voice and body. When you pause, you give the body a chance to settle and re-establish a grounded state. It's a quick way to focus your attention inwardly and make sure the body is open and forward.

In an Executive World

Below are some of the more common situations and challenges that executives face with commitment and involvement, and a few of the techniques we use to improve their skills.

Compelling Messages: It's hard to be compelling when your message isn't great. We spend a lot of time on messaging and helping executives think through what a group should take away. Spoken communication doesn't drive a lot of detail; close to 90% of the content is quickly forgotten. But, messages can have a lasting impact and when executives feel their messages are compelling, it's much easier to deliver them.

We encourage executives to get the core message across in a single sentence. It becomes the tagline or bottom line of the entire presentation. Once they understand the role and impact of a message, it's very easy to keep them on point and following a storyline in a presentation.

Reach the Back Row: I mentioned before that a change in audience size can diminish an executive's presence. When the setting is unfamiliar, I see executives try to draw off the portion of the room they're comfortable with by focusing on only the first ten rows or one side of a room. This can quickly divide a group or alienate the back row. We teach executives how to pull in an entire room. It requires the use of all the coachable skills, but voice is the most critical.

It's important to learn that the front row is usually full of the best listeners. No one has to work very hard for that group. Those who are keeping their distance and sitting in the back of the room will be the bigger challenge to engage. This is easy to consider when you are live with a group, and harder to manage when the audience is remote.

When we rehearse in large rooms we show executives how to divide it into quadrants and find three or four points of connection in each quadrant. This ensures they are reaching the entire audience and helps pull their energy and focus to different places.

Remote Audiences: Every executive will face remote audiences. It's important to know what changes occur within your own style and presence because of this medium. It's a harder setup for both speakers and listeners. You can improve the energy level of the call which adds to presence, but you can't duplicate the physical component. For this reason, we also work on content for remote presentations to be sure the right choice is made about when to talk to groups remotely and when you need to be physically present.

A general guideline is to use live meetings for new strategies and significant changes. Remote presentations are better for reinforcing ideas that groups have already heard. Remote presentations also work best with audiences who already know the executive or speaker. It's much easier for the voice to reinforce an impression than to establish a new one.

Coaching Others on Commitment & Involvement

The voice is a hard skill to coach and most executives are tentative and reluctant to explore this. Avoid trying to guide someone through techniques of the voice if you aren't familiar with how to do so. But, you can reinforce some of the concepts below that often free the voice easily.

Mumblers: If you work with an executive who mumbles, you can tell them it doesn't sound as if they mean what they're saying. Encourage them to try to convince the group or get a reaction to their message. "You need to really say it like you mean it." As people think about working harder, it often helps them open the mouth more naturally.

Fast Talkers: The best way to slow down a fast talker is to encourage them to pause. If someone is working from a written text, it's easy to mark scripts or teleprompters for pauses. If they're speaking from an outline, make sure the beginning is very deliberate in pace. The pace of speaking is set in the first few minutes, so if you can get someone to pause for emphasis in the beginning, most will hold onto the concept of pausing as they move through the content.

The Dreaded Ums: The use of "ums" and "likes" is devastating to executive presence. It creates a casual impression and can appear as if the speaker doesn't know his point. Most people who do this tend to ramble. Speakers use filler to link thoughts and often end up with four or five sentences running all together. We actually speak in sound bites and can eliminate filler by coaching an executive to speak in phrases instead of sentences. This is also an important technique for media training.

Phone Posture: Posture is an important part of a stand-up presentation but it also matters on the phone. The voice is the only tool executives have to create impressions over the phone, and most are more effective if they stand to speak on conference calls or remote presentations. When you stand, it's easier to project the voice and gain full use of the diaphragm for breath support.

Tricky Words: I haven't met an executive who doesn't struggle with some words. If you support the writing or message development of an executive, you should know what his or her tough words are. It may be poor pronunciation, variation of accents, or blended sounds. It doesn't matter why the word is tricky; it just isn't worth the risk of asking the executive to say it. When I draft manuscript speeches, my first step in rehearsal is to listen for tricky words. Then, I eliminate every one of them. While it may diminish the impact of the meaning slightly, that's nothing in comparison to what tricky words do to undermine an executive's confidence. The delivery far outweighs word choice.

Once the core skills of body and voice are improved, learning how to engage a group adds the differentiating factor.

12

Coachable Skill - Engagement

If there is a magical aspect to communication, engagement is it. In any workshop or discussion of effective communication skills, we ask people to describe a good communicator. Inevitably, the adjectives used have a lot to do with how a speaker makes the listeners feel. People describe this idea of engagement as honesty, openness, and transparency. Most say the speaker cares about the listener's reaction.

If you review our Hierarchy of Attributes (Chapter 3), these are the differentiating qualities that elicit emotion. Our survey respondents described engagement as believable, authentic, empathetic, and transparent. Essentially, engagement is the skill that shifts attention away from the executive and onto the listener or audience.

I tell executives this is the skill that can't be faked, and it takes time to master. Being an engaged communicator requires being an effective listener. It shifts thoughts away from how the speaker is seen to how the listener is responding. It is an honest desire to connect with people and to make an impact with a compelling message.

Vulnerability & Authenticity

I opened this book with a reference to the fairy tale about the emperor with no clothes. It stands to reason that this skill of engagement can make someone feel "naked" or vulnerable in front of a group. But, it's the very concept of being open that also makes people seem authentic. I don't think audiences always expect the right answer, but they do expect an honest one. For most leaders, trying to be honest leaves them feeling a little vulnerable.

While the skills of physical presence and commitment were about the impressions of voice and body, the skill of engagement is about intent. Our goal is to help an executive understand the intent of engagement and to develop the skills that raise awareness of others and insights into reactions.

The Conversation

I coached an executive once who was totally surprised to hear that he needed to think about connecting with listeners. We had worked on some of the fundamentals of voice and body, and I told him I wanted to talk to him about his impact on a group. He looked at me with astonishment and said, "What do you mean by impact?" I told him I wanted to raise his awareness of perceptions and reactions.

He was surprised to hear I thought he should be focused on reactions. He said, "For twenty-five years I've walked into meetings and given people my ideas. In fact, you could say I load up my knowledge and dump it in reports and updates to pass it along. I've never once thought about how it was received or that it was my job to deliver it in a way that welcomed input and solicited feedback."

While his reaction may seem surprising, it isn't uncommon. Many coaching candidates are shocked to hear that coaching will be more about their audiences than about them.

Most of us connect in our personal communication; we just don't think about it in a business setting. That's because in conversation it's easy to create a two-way dialogue or connection. In business settings, the connection becomes more of an acknowledgement of a listener and awareness of non-verbal reactions. The challenge is knowing how to engage consistently across all communication situations.

Start with the Strengths

I begin work on this skill by figuring out where someone is most engaging. I ask questions about work settings, personal relationships, and one-on-one conversations, to uncover the more comfortable skills. This period of discovery happens through role-plays, observation, and honest discussion. Then, I try to compare a more authentic style against some of the roadblocks that exist in business environments. If I can help an executive see they already display some of the qualities it takes to engage a listener, then it's simply a matter of getting comfortable using the same skills in other situations.

I'll never forget a woman who was very polished, but stiff, in her approach. There was no doubt she was credible, but it was hard to see any warmth or interest on her part. I tried talking about the listeners' needs, sharing feedback, and impressions, but I just couldn't break the tough exterior. Then, I began asking about her personal experiences. I found a point of connection with her from my own background. I shared my experience, and it made her comfortable enough to open up about herself. As she shared with me, she became more open and conversational. The contrast between her corporate self and her more conversational self was eye-opening to her. It gave her a glimpse of how she wanted to be seen, and we had a clear direction for coaching.

Pulling In vs. Pushing Out

Most of us move up through organizations waiting for the moment when someone will begin to listen to us. It's very true the world has few natural listeners; we're all just waiting for our opportunity to speak. I observe executives and managers every week who are pushing information out just as fast and furious as they can. They have a lot to say and demand the respect to be heard.

Yet, the concept of engagement is more about pulling people in rather than pushing information out. The idea of "pushing out" doesn't put any responsibility on the speaker to make sure the information is received and valued. In fact, most listeners forget about 90% of the spoken words they hear. So, if the speaker doesn't take responsibility for pulling them into ideas, chances are slim they'll walk away with much of anything.

We use a number of exercises to illustrate the idea of pulling the listener to you rather than pushing information out. The idea is to get speakers thinking about impact, buy-in, and persuasion. It's the desire to connect and engage every listener.

Working for Reactions & Reading Non-Verbal Cues

In coaching, we shift expectations about successful communication away from how the speaker felt, to the speaker's impact and what the listeners heard. Ultimately, great engagement comes from a heightened awareness of non-verbal cues and reactions. People with presence focus on making something happen rather than getting through scripted words. They have the ability to read the room and react to it in order to influence a group.

We coach this skill by working on active listening, heightening awareness of non-verbal cues, and building awareness of every listener. We often shadow executives to offer insights on reactions and small group dynamics. Our goal is to raise awareness of engagement on a daily basis so that it's easier to deliver it under pressure. It's the hardest of the coachable skills to master and the most effective of the skills in front of any group.

In an Executive World

Being Open & Honest: In today's pressured communication situations, it's easy to say you want to be open, but it can be hard to execute. I differentiate between openness in style and openness with content. Executives tell me all the time that they can't tell employees everything about a merger or a layoff on a given day. I tell them that being honest about limitations is the first step. Your personal style can put a group at ease long before your content. Audiences don't expect to know everything, but they do expect to be able to trust what they are being told. It's important for an executive to understand what qualities they exemplify around openness and then to help them replicate those across all speaking situations, especially the tough ones!

Storytelling: Telling great stories is a wonderful way to help an executive connect with an audience. It can also be a revealing one. Too often, I work on speeches that sound flat in delivery, especially when it comes to the stories. When this occurs I'll stop an executive to ask about the story. Usually, they tell me they don't know the story or the person mentioned in it. My advice is to take the story out.

Stories should be authentic. An audience can tell a fake story a mile away. Stories are compelling and they can be a great way to share personal experiences. But, they have to be real to the speaker and used in a way that creates a compelling message for the audience.

We work with people to help them learn how to tell stories well. Stories can bridge a level of detail and complexity, they can pull a diverse audience together, and they often help put the listeners into a situation or an opportunity.

Humor: We're often asked to help executives use humor to connect. That's a coaching goal I try to avoid. When someone asks me to create a funny opening for them, I ask, "Are you a funny person?" Often, the answer is no. I explain that humor is all about timing. Funny people can make the most mundane situation funny because of their timing. The idea of wanting to connect from the very beginning is a good one. We can help anyone become a good storyteller, but comedic timing is best learned in a comedy club.

The Open Forum & Tough Questions: Communication has become so constant that the idea of "protecting" leaders from certain audiences is just not realistic. Twenty years ago, a top executive would pick the forum of his choice and limit the way in which he or she engaged with a group. One common format that leaders like to avoid is an open forum with undefined questions from employees or external groups. Avoiding this format is just not feasible in today's high impact setting with so many diverse audiences. It's critical for all executives to feel confident handling an open forum and thinking on their feet. There will be more on this in Chapter 17.

Coaching Others on Engagement

The Speechwriter's Challenge: Since content and style establish connection for a speaker, it's often the speechwriter who gets blamed when the speech is flat or the speaker doesn't connect with a group. While the content can miss opportunities for connection, the blame can't fully fall on a speechwriter. Even the best speechwriter can't improvise on the personal touches.

We help many executives learn how to work with writers. Great messages are a combination of personal touch and anecdotes with a broader context and overall direction. Good writers can help you frame-up a concept and explore different ways to present a topic.

Avoid Feedback on Eye Contact & Techniques: True engagement is a process rather than a technique. Many executives come to us frustrated because they've worked for years on eye contact and are still getting feedback that they aren't open and honest. It takes a number of different concepts and an executive's own self-discovery to become more engaging. It takes an experienced coach to help someone shift their focus beyond techniques to true connection.

Share Impressions & Reactions: The better feedback for an executive who needs to engage a group is to share your observations and impressions of how an audience responded. Feedback is the best way to raise awareness of engagement. Soliciting evaluations of presentations or reviewing videotaped presentations can help many executives understand impressions.

Content vs. Contact: Engagement happens through messaging as well as style. If an executive is struggling with style, you can help him gain connection with content. Ultimately, the two aspects work together, and those who learn to connect with content will become more open with their style.

The Conversational Tone: You can also help an executive explore a conversational tone. If you are working with someone who seems stiff or formal on their feet, ask them to sit down and simply talk to you about the topic. Try to illustrate the difference in the formal delivery and the conversational approach. Many executives can bring warmth to their delivery with this comparison.

13

The Right Time for Coaching

The previous chapters have focused on how we help executives gain presence. While many of the examples focus on individual coaching scenarios, we also work with companies to build effective leadership programs and develop future leaders.

In fact, the executives we surveyed and interviewed ranked these programs as one of the top ways to gain presence. Many succession discussions and development programs debate the ideal time to develop presence. Some say it should wait until an employee is far enough along in his or her career to really command a presence; others say every middle manager should get feedback about impressions and their ability to influence others.

I agree with the latter. All of the executives we interviewed got feedback early in their careers and set out early to make an impression.

The survey input suggests that mid-management becomes the point of differentiation. While many executives felt middle managers in their company were valued for technical skills, all felt it was hard to get beyond a middle management level without a sense of presence and the ability to engage others. The challenge becomes understanding the balance point at which presence can help someone get ahead versus the lack of presence holding someone back.

One executive said, "It's a shame that we don't take the time to really understand people's abilities and to measure everyone's aptitude. But, the truth is it just takes too long to get to know someone when they aren't working hard to help you. We rely heavily on impressions and reactions from others.

"You can walk into any mid-level meeting within our company and see presence at work. You don't need to know names or positions. Within fifteen minutes, you can spot our future leaders by watching who others are listening to."

What's the Right Time for Coaching?

Timing should first be based on awareness. If you have employees on a high potential list or in a leadership development program, you owe them a thorough assessment. If you're going to single out managers for development and ask the managers to put in additional time to accelerate skills, the managers deserve to know what they're doing well and what they need to learn to do better.

Presence is a coachable skill but it is rarely a self-identified one. This is because it relies heavily on impressions. As mentioned in Chapter 9, we use a number of tools to interpret impressions and to help someone understand perceptions.

In high potential programs we recommend offering an assessment and an introduction to coachable skills. As many executives said, observation had one of the greatest impacts on their skills. Raising awareness for a middle-level manager is a powerful start to begin thinking about presenting ideas with confidence and credibility.

The other important element of development is convincing managers that timing is everything. Everyone gets a chance, but the timing of that chance is unpredictable.

It may be part of a leadership program and fairly obvious to managers that they are being observed. Or, the big moment may take a manager completely by surprise on the one day he or she didn't really take the time to prepare for a meeting.

While the executives we surveyed all felt there was a big moment in their careers, they didn't leave it to chance. All of them said they prepared for every meeting and considered every setting to be an opportunity. That takes a lot of work, but for the group we interviewed, it certainly paid off.

We recommend that all mid-level managers get exposure to presence. This allows a company to raise the bar on expectations and set the groundwork for on-going feedback. Then, as opportunities expand, it's beneficial for more seasoned managers to get individual coaching.

Coaching allows a manager to fine-tune his individual skills and gain the insights and expertise needed to strengthen them. While it can take years for a manager to develop presence, we can accelerate the process in a matter of months. We do this through situational coaching which allows us to coach fundamentals and then help an individual apply those skills to specific situations.

Ultimately, we help individuals strengthen impressions and build a powerful presence. It's easier to build impressions than to change them and that's really the answer to the ideal timing. For any manager, the right time for coaching is the point at which presence can help them get ahead and not hold them back.

The final section of the book highlights some of the most common communication challenges in today's business environment and the insights we've used to help leaders bring an executive presence to each of them.

Section 3:

Applying Presence in Today's Business Environment

14

Communication in the C-Suite

While I've discussed the ideal time for coaching and the point at which executive presence can accelerate or stall a career, there is no doubt that C-Suite positions are rarely reached without it. You've read stories and quotes from leaders who have shared their experiences in developing presence in themselves and others. Now, I'll share my experiences in supporting top-level executives and the role of communication specifically in the C-Suite.

In one out of every three executive coaching assignments we take on, the executive is genuinely surprised things aren't going smoothly. After all, most of them have given hundreds of presentations and dealt with many different audiences through the years. My response is always, "Nothing is the same, and the skills that worked last week have now been pushed to the next level."

Communication coaching is a very common step when a seasoned manager or executive is promoted to the C-Suite. Three factors drive this: impact, time, and feedback.

The impact and dynamics of communication skyrocket in C-Suite roles. Even the most confident executives are a little unnerved as the audiences get bigger, the messages get broader, and the expectations soar. Time becomes a challenge because there are more communication demands and opportunities and less time to prepare for them. Third, feedback shuts down. While most CEOs have a few close confidants within a company, it is harder to get an honest critique and therefore to measure impact.

The shift in communication dynamics and expectations may seem unfair, but it is very real and has lasting implications. My initial conversations with C-Suite executives often focus on understanding that their role as a communicator has shifted from one who outlines next steps to one who sets overall strategy and direction. Content shifts from clear details to broader ideas and vision.

Personal style skills are placed under close observation. Audiences form quick impressions of all of us when we stand up to speak. For a C-Suite executive, there is little distinction between an initial impression and a lasting one. When a middle manager speaks at a company-wide meeting, he may lack energy or focus as he delivers his thoughts. While it doesn't do much to motivate the audience, he still has the opportunity to sit down with his group and reinforce his ideas in a smaller setting. For the C-Suite executive, it's more of a one shot approach. When he lacks energy or focus, the audience holds onto that impression for six months to a year until they see him again in the same setting.

Time is a critical factor because many executives experience a tremendous shift in the amount of time it takes to develop and deliver messages. While seasoned managers spend on average about 35-40% of their time preparing and delivering key messages, top executives should be spending 60-65% of their time on communication. In fact, I often begin a coaching engagement with a simple calculation to figure out how much time goes into developing messages and influencing audiences. If this amount represents less than 50% of an executive's time, I'm willing to bet there's a distressed communications group behind him.

Feedback on communication, presence, and impact is a slippery slope. Who wants to go on record telling the CEO he's boring or uninspiring? I still remember an experience over ten years ago. I was asked by an EVP of communications to observe a meeting. I didn't get a lot of background and was told that he just wanted to talk to me afterwards about my impressions. So, I attended the meeting and sat in the back row to observe the top three executives of the company. Afterwards, I joined the EVP for lunch and I asked, "Why am I here?" He didn't skip a beat as he said, "Because I can fire you if they don't like your input."

That's one way to think about the value of an outside coach!

While it isn't part of every coaching engagement, I often talk about a personal communication plan. A personal plan can help an executive map out how and when communication will occur. It can also set a proactive direction, tone, and theme to communication that ensures consistency across meetings and presentations and makes it much easier for others to support executive communication.

It's probably not surprising that most executives use speechwriters, but it may be surprising to know that they don't all use writers effectively. Most executives work better with one resource than several. What an executive really wants a speechwriter to do is outline his thoughts and perspective and create a framework for the ideas that makes it interesting enough to follow and intriguing enough to remember. Not an easy task!

As a communication coach, I often work with the executive and his or her speechwriter to help fine-tune the delivery of ideas and ensure the executive will be able to bring them to life.

A communication plan helps prioritize key audiences, consistent messages, and best platforms. As we gathered input on presence and communication through the survey and interviews, we talked to many executives about communication challenges. Many respondents said that how to communicate was the primary concern.

So many different methods of communication exist today. They range from live speeches and meetings to webcasts and podcasts, and from texting and tweeting to emails and voicemails. For an executive, it can be overwhelming trying to use and master all of them. Interestingly, all of our current clients are working on expanding their confidence with a diversity of platforms.

As one executive said, "When I first became CEO I usually had a surprise element, something special to announce when I spoke to an audience. It just isn't that way anymore. Real-time communication makes it impossible to keep much under wraps. So, I can't rely on anticipation anymore. I feel the pressure to inspire and interpret more these days."

Common Trends

While every role is different, there are common trends I see among executives who leverage communication in the C-Suite. If you are new to the role or want to increase your impact, consider the following:

Create Your Personal Communication Plan: It ought to be a part of every new CEO's thirty-day plan. Define core messages and initial direction and spell out how and when you plan to communicate these. This is one of the most impactful impressions you can create with all of your key audiences. It says you care about them and plan to talk to them often.

Open Up Personally: Audiences love stories and examples, and they love to feel connected to executives and leaders. But don't make the classic mistake of just telling stories. It's the personal touch that people love. Executives miss the mark by adding stories they haven't actually experienced. From the very beginning, be real and honest with your content. This allows it to help position your presence and style.

Personal stories are not self promotion. I coach executives to use stories to relate to the group, and we work hard to make sure a connection exists. There are many different ways to tell stories but the most effective is to be sure your audience relates to the experience. So rather than telling your story about being named the MVP on the soccer team when there might be only one person in the audience who relates to the story, tell the story of working hard to learn how to play soccer including what it took to be a good team player, the highs and lows of practice, etc. Chances are more than half of your audience can relate to that story.

Lose the Visuals & Support Materials: Top executives create vision, strategy, and future direction. Visuals support details. If you're still giving audiences a lot of detail and tactics, you're still in the manager's role. So, while PowerPoint may have a place in the boardroom, the use of visuals should be significantly reduced in executive messages. C-Suite executives shift from high content to high contact.

Seek Feedback: Nobody's perfect, but everyone can be effective. It's true that everyone stops talking to you when you reach the C-Suite. There are just too many risks associated with being honest with the boss. Executives need feedback, especially new executives, to be sure they're connecting with audiences. Some even bring trusted advisors with them to the C-Suite. Others find coaches who help provide insight and perspective on senior-level communication.

The timing of coaching often coincides with the move to the C-Suite and it turns out to be a great time for support. Coaching provides the opportunity for an executive to develop new habits and gain confidence in the ability to connect with larger audiences, define broader messages, and exceed expectations in front of any group.

15

Define & Expand Your Audiences

In the last chapter we talked about audiences getting bigger and executives focusing on how to reach a broader range of people. Chapter 17 will address the methods and platforms of communication, but this chapter gives thought to the kinds of audiences you need exposure to in order to reach a senior-level position.

For years, people assumed that sales and marketing roles were the more high profile positions and led to the more visible opportunities. Today, you see CFOs moving to the C-Suite and administrators and analysts getting a seat at the table.

While these roles may bring good business acumen, they don't bring the experience and exposure with diverse audiences. It can be a daunting challenge as you step into your new role. Instead, if you think about becoming exposed to diverse audiences while still in your current role, it can be an opportunity to gain experience and therefore be better prepared and more appealing as a senior-level candidate.

More than once I've received input on a coaching candidate that goes like this, "He is really well respected and admired within our organization. The biggest challenge our CFO has is that he comes across as a CFO." I could repeat that quote for many senior-level positions. When you're good at what you do, you are often stereotyped. The very thing that got you ahead may be the very attribute that holds you back. The challenge is being seen as successful in your current role but promotable to the next. Broad exposure to different places can expand those perceptions.

When you step into a senior role, you'll soon see that no one can learn how to do everything in the first 100 days. Unfortunately, most of the audiences listed below will expect some kind of interaction. The more exposure you've had to them in advance, the easier it will be to step into the spotlight and command a presence.

Below are the key audiences we focus on and thoughts on how to get exposure if you're not in front of them already.

EMPLOYEES: This group provides your internal "approval rating" and is often neglected as executives deal with customer pressures and industry exposure. In our survey, senior leaders rated this as the audience they worry about the most. Employees have to stay motivated and engaged or nothing else really matters. This isn't a tough group to get in front of, yet 62% of the leaders we surveyed worry more about impressions and presence with this audience than any other. See the survey results in the appendix at the end of the book.

For leaders, it's about creating the kind of forum employees like best. They want to see executives and feel as if they have access to them. Big company meetings are a great idea and should happen a few times a year. But these don't replace informal environments that allow employees to truly interact with leaders. Employees love the exposure and leaders will find this type of interaction yields more accurate information than any employee survey can.

HAVEN'T SPOKEN TO THIS GROUP? Training for the "company-wide" meeting can happen for any seasoned manager. While you may not have access to all employees, you are constantly part of a group of some employees. Learn how to talk to this group and volunteer to give reports and updates, or lead discussions so that you gain experience in soliciting input from co-workers. You'll find in short order that you're often asked to speak to internal groups. Many managers hate doing this so there's always an available spot.

PEERS: Everyone presents to their peer group, but few focus on its significance. Even among peers it is evident who the true leaders are and a group will begin to treat them as such. Peer groups are a great audience for learning how to establish a sense of confidence and engagement. You should know the reactions and non-verbal cues of your peers well.

One development leader said, "When we develop leaders, we really need to develop them as a small community rather than individuals. After all, they're going to be a future team that has to work together." I think that's very true.

HAVEN'T SPOKEN TO THIS GROUP? You need to speak up! If you're not getting equal time in peer meetings, you need to do something about it. Even if you are running projects that don't impact the entire group, this is the place to take an interest in what others are doing and offer input and insights outside of your own responsibilities.

CUSTOMERS: The executives surveyed said this was the second most important audience. One of the best ways to understand your company is to see it through the eyes of the customer. Those in sales and marketing have long had the advantage with this group, but this gap is easy to remedy by taking more interest in how customers engage with your company.

We work on many large client conferences, and I'm always intrigued to see how the CEO and the head of sales participate in the meeting. Usually, the CEO opens the conference and sets an industry-focused vision and direction for the company and then the head of sales talks more specifically about the year ahead and new tactics to help client businesses.

But, within the last year, we worked with two companies where the CEO took a back seat at the meeting. In one instance, he wasn't comfortable speaking and didn't really know the customer base. In the second instance, he was too focused on a potential acquisition and wasn't even planning to attend the conference.

I stood beside the first CEO as the head of sales delivered the vision presentation we had helped create. The CEO turned to me and said, "I think I made a mistake." And, he was right. Within eighteen months the head of sales had his job.

In the second instance, the company experienced challenges with product roll-outs shortly after the conference. I was involved in helping develop some of the key messages and knew that consistent feedback from the field showed customers felt the CEO wasn't as focused as he should be on the new products because he didn't even show up at the conference to talk about them. That was another costly mistake.

HAVEN'T SPOKEN TO THIS GROUP? Attend client conferences where all your customers are together. Offer to be a speaker to add your expertise to the client agenda. Jump in when you hear of client challenges and offer to be part of a difficult meeting. From the client's perspective, they are always interested in meeting others in a company and learning about a different dimension of the business.

Even without speaking to customers this is a perspective you should have. Try to attend the conferences they attend, read the periodicals they read, and expand your knowledge to include a good understanding of what the industry and others within it are discussing.

MEDIA: This is the "feared" audience and can be the acid test for advancement to the C-Level. This group is viewed as tough, aggressive, and often out to get you. That's really not true, although the media is often the most prepared audience you will experience. In our media workshops, we teach managers and executives how to prepare for interviews so that you shift from a responsive role to a proactive one.

We coach many media interviews and the difference I see between someone who is ready for an intensive interview and someone who isn't has a lot to do with the person's training and experience to date. In a pressured situation, you can count on public relations and communication experts to help create and refine messages. But, it's difficult to help an executive learn how to answer questions well when the pressure is on.

Interestingly, this group came in fourth in our survey with only 52% of executives saying they work hardest to have presence with the media. This is because the exposure is not as frequent as with the other audiences. But access to the media is changing and my advice to companies is to expose executives and rising leaders to media situations early in their careers. The face of the media has changed so much that it doesn't take an interview on *60 Minutes* to gain experience and learn how to communicate key messages.

Media now includes bloggers, Twitter enthusiasts, conference attendees, industry publishers, web surfers, etc. The best way to prepare executives for big, pressured moments is to make sure they have lots of little ones.

HAVEN'T SPOKEN TO THIS GROUP? The diversity of media today presents many opportunities. Whether you call it a media interview or just a Q&A session, there are opportunities to talk to public groups at trade shows, customer conferences, and industry events. Putting yourself in Q&A situations will help you practice giving clear and concise responses and using stories and examples to support your ideas. It's also never too soon to go through a media training program to understand how to answer questions and how to balance your perspective with that of a journalist.

INDUSTRY & FINANCIAL ANALYSTS: Analysts are considered by some to be the same audience as the media, but the objectives are so different it's important to consider them separately. While analysts, too, are one of the most prepared audiences you will get in front of, an analyst is looking for data and trends while a journalist is building a story. We prepare executives for these two audiences very differently.

Talking to an analyst is very much a financial game, and it's often more a strength of the CFO than the CEO. But, this audience usually demands to hear from both. As companies have moved toward remote analyst updates and calls, we've done a lot of work to support this new format and to help ensure messages are as impactful remotely as they are in person.

HAVEN'T SPOKEN TO THIS GROUP? You're not likely to unless you're coming up through the financial division. But, most analyst calls are published and it's easy enough to listen to what your company is saying on these calls. Familiarity with the context of analyst discussions and the kinds of questions they ask would be a good first step to becoming more confident with financial data. Lack of business acumen or financial savvy is one of the biggest worries companies have about future leaders. This would be a smart way to close that gap.

BOARD MEMBERS: At the C-Level, board members are a critical audience. You wouldn't be in front of this group if you didn't have a sense of presence about you. For many top executives, this audience is a difficult one because your exposure may be limited to a formal setting. The CEO usually has the stronger relationship and should since he reports to the Board. But your future is in their hands as well, and it's critical to make sure that each impression in front of this group is a good one.

I work with many senior executives to improve the quality of their board presentations. The Board receives a lot of information, and it can be difficult to figure out what they really want to hear and how to drive a clear message through all the information. I've worked with many executives who didn't want to change up the current approach, and yet when we did, it always got noticed.

You may not realize how involved most Boards are in assessments and impressions of the entire leadership team. When we begin a coaching engagement with a C-Level executive, we are usually given impressions from the Board. As you think about advancement within a company, rarely does someone step into a top leadership role if they haven't had exposure to the Board.

HAVEN'T SPOKEN TO THIS GROUP? This is a hard audience to gain access to until the time is right. More and more companies are putting seasoned managers in front of this group to give them early exposure and to give the Board more "in the trenches" information. This opportunity will be an important one, and you should seize the moment if it comes your way. These impressions will last and we've coached many a seasoned manager on how to make the most of this high visibility event. Interestingly, the managers in the finance department are more likely to get this opportunity.

COMMUNITY: Most leaders are expected to be active in the community and depending on their business this will either be local involvement or more national in scope. Wherever the company is trying to make an impact, senior leaders are often asked to speak to community groups. These groups have always been seen as fairly "risk-free," although with the vast increase in information across the web, these audiences are more informed and involved than they used to be.

Two clients shared experiences from community speeches that they were surprised by and unprepared to address.

One communications director prepared his CEO for a local community speech. The speech went fine until they got to Q&A. It turns out their company was dealing with some union negotiations halfway around the world. A member of the audience was from that part of the world and kept up with news through an online newspaper. He stood up and asked a question about something that hadn't been in the US news at all. They were caught flat-footed.

Another executive was dealing with a security issue within her company the morning of her talk. The breach had occurred three hours before the speech. The national media hadn't picked up on it and the company was preparing a statement for that afternoon, but someone in her audience had read about it on a blog. She was shocked at how quickly information got out.

A community audience has become a more informed audience. We encourage executives to pick a topic when speaking to a community group and stick to it. Some of the challenges occur when the topics get too broad and content has to be reinvented for every community audience. Read more about this in Chapter 16.

HAVEN'T SPOKEN TO THIS GROUP? Community leadership provides a great opportunity to gain confidence as a speaker and visibility within a community. This is a great way to groom future leaders, and some companies build community roles into the development plans of their high potential managers. The best way to leverage this involvement is to be very active in one or two things rather than trying to get your name on several boards and not having the time to make an impact on any of them.

Expanding your exposure to key audiences is a critical part of being an effective communicator and leader. The more audiences you understand, the more likely you will be able to engage them. Our coaching relationships always begin with a discussion of key audiences.

One way that high potential and current leaders gain exposure to these audiences is by becoming a thought leader which is the topic of our next chapter.

16

Position Yourself as a Thought Leader

Thought leadership has become a buzz word in recent years as companies strive to differentiate themselves in their industry. Small companies think it's a strategy industry leaders are using to tout their R&D departments. Some view it as a way to stake out the future; yet others see it as owning the current market. Everyone is right. Thought leadership is a concept that covers all of this.

Ultimately, it's the new sales pitch. The smarter customer is demanding more than a product. They want a relationship and a knowledge resource. In response, many companies are transitioning their way of selling to talk more about how they think, rather than just about what they offer. Thought leadership for a company centers around the brand promise and what you're telling customers about your company.

Thought leadership as a business strategy can be complicated as companies shift the way they meet the marketplace. If companies are ultimately going to move toward a thought leadership strategy then it stands to reason that somewhere within the company they will have to have thought leaders. Long before companies can get there, individual leaders can.

These leaders aren't defined by a title or position; they could be a manager in the IT department or a vice president of finance.

To us, thought leadership simply means differentiating yourself and becoming knowledgeable enough on a topic that audiences seek you as the speaker rather than your company. It's landing on a topic or an area of focus within your industry and investing the time to become a valued resource and advisor. This is a critical way that senior managers build an executive presence outside of their companies and often accelerate their career by becoming known within an industry and sought after as a resource.

There is a huge communication component to thought leadership. Every month, executives stand in front of customers and external audiences and talk about strategies and the positioning of new products. In all of these presentations we tell executives that they gain more credibility by talking through issues and external situations than by giving details of a product solution.

Every week, we develop messages and presentations and send executives out to their external audiences to deliver them. Yet I'm always amazed at the missed opportunities. Presentations deliver great ideas and insights. However, once it's said, it's forgotten. Time and effort goes into creating powerful messages and rarely are presentations repeated or leveraged as part of an overall communication strategy.

We coach executives to leverage topics and audiences. If you're going to invest time to talk at conferences and industry groups, then also invest the time to become a valued source on a topic. Pick your area of interest and learn it backwards and forwards. Corporate communications groups are always trying to develop speakers beyond the CEO. They would be more than happy to have another resource to propose to groups and can easily leverage a thought leader and their topic within the industry. We work with many corporate communication teams to develop high profile thought leaders and the impact of this effort is impressive.

When asked about developing future speakers, one corporate communications leader told me that she had quite by accident "discovered" a young employee who was very effective. As part of a media story, a journalist asked to talk to younger employees who might have a different perspective for her story. The communications leader asked around within the company and was directed to a young man who worked in one of the regional offices. She prepped him for a small part in the interview and was amazed at how well he presented himself and his thoughts. Now she calls on him frequently as a thought leader on the topic. That was definitely a high profile moment for the young manager.

Three steps to consider as you think about defining yourself as a thought leader:

1. Understand Your Customer & Your Industry: Most thought leaders gain attention by defining the market in a way no one else has. They see something differently or are exploring it from a different angle. You don't have to create a new product, you simply have to be willing to talk about challenges and invest time in studying these challenges.

2. Define What You Know & What Interests You: Executives tell us they simply don't know enough about certain topics to talk to other industry leaders about them. Don't try to know everything; just know something very well. Then be willing to share your thoughts and observations constantly. Give away your knowledge with reckless abandon in publications, customer conferences, white papers, trade journals, etc.

3. Align with a Signature Solution: As you become a thought leader, you will begin to talk about solutions rather than specific products. A signature solution should tie back to your company, but it is rarely an advertisement for it. Make yourself an advocate rather than a commercial.

Three steps to consider as you develop a communications strategy for your topic:

Once you land on a topic, you need to think through a communication strategy to support it. For many leaders, this is a key part of the communication plan we discussed in Chapter 14. As you build a strategy, consider these three steps:

1. Create It: This is not your typical presentation. This is a mind-shifting message. You want to provoke, surprise, and engage an audience. And, you need to leave them wanting more. Invest the time and energy to get this right, so you will feel confident and excited about delivering it again and again.

You'll need a strong message with good insights and examples to bring your concepts to life. As you get started, you may not have insights of your own. You can use research, white papers, and other trusted sources for data. But, you will need an idea about the topic that is centered around your own unique point of view.

A few years ago, we worked with an executive who was chosen by his company as the sustainability expert. The company was just beginning to explore sustainability and knew they needed to have a voice within the industry. The only challenge was that this executive didn't know anything about sustainability nor did he have experience in the area. He would gain experience over the next several months as he stepped into the new role, but they were eager for him to speak sooner and he didn't have anything to say.

We developed a unique angle for him from the consumers' perspective, and his presentation was a hit. As his knowledge grew, his presentation evolved and within twelve months he was one of the most sought after sustainability speakers within his industry. He has also advanced two levels within the organization in the three years we've known him.

Consider this: The average presentation takes about three days of development time from an executive. Then, it only lives for sixty minutes. Imagine a presentation that is delivered twelve times and lives for months within an industry. That's a leveraged plan.

2. Sustain It: Once you develop it, you've got to sustain the message. Not only by repeating the presentation itself, but through a communication plan that builds on the ideas and creates repetition around them. Some executives do this internally with monthly phone updates and internal newsletters. However, most concepts stop short of external communication which actually allows the thought leadership to build within an industry.

You have to consistently provide cutting-edge information and answers through external newsletters, conferences, or articles. Visibility is an essential component of positioning yourself as a recognizable expert. Unlike self-promotion and the guy we all view as a political player, thought leadership adds value to the listener and advances discussion on critical topics.

A great example of this is the investment world where money managers create their own persona through newsletters, blogs, and industry appearances.

3. Expand It: A communication strategy behind thought leadership allows for broader support in positioning a topic and an individual. Often, key messages can grow into other topics or gain relevance in other industries. A team effort can help an executive expand an idea and keep a topic fresh or leverage it to broader audiences.

Here's how I've seen it work. An executive came to us for help developing a message about recycling benefits. He was actually in the property management business and his firm had taken some heat about not recycling on large properties. He was developing a board presentation to drive a decision on whether or not they should consider recycling.

As we gathered data and research for his presentation, he was surprised by the statistics we uncovered and became intrigued with the possibilities. His presentation shifted from simply explaining options to seeking buy-in for a comprehensive recycling program.

He used the same presentation to show his plan to each of his property managers and his team created a recycling campaign so that tenants would recognize it. He tracked the results and followed up with the key audiences to prove that the assumptions he laid out in the initial presentation were reached. His insights were noticed.

He was asked to present the project and its results at Property Management conferences. His firm won a national award for the campaign and he started a quarterly newsletter covering their efforts.

In short order, he created it, expanded it, and is now sustaining it with the help of his communication team. He is seen as a thought leader on recycling and has been interviewed, quoted, and recognized many times for his insights on recycling. As an added benefit, their occupancy rates have climbed as well.

Thought leadership can happen inside or outside a company. It can be a major undertaking or just an added component of a well thought out communication plan. Either way, thought leadership is a powerful tool to leverage visibility. The more you're seen, the more likely you are to establish an executive presence with all of your key audiences. And, being seen is one communication method that many executives forget.

17

Be Seen as Well as Heard

I mentioned in a previous chapter that many executives are struggling with the various communication platforms they've been presented. In our business we see a vast difference between those who are managing outlets effectively and those who are struggling.

From social media to remote communication to written context and live discussions, executives are harried trying to be all things to all people. We've seen those who have retreated and only work within communication settings they're comfortable with, and we've seen those who are trying to span it all and send the word out across all platforms.

It's easy to get pulled under by a communication world that runs 24/7. I've observed the pressures of trying to stay on top of it all and still bring authenticity and thoughtfulness to every message.

I sat in a meeting with a senior communications leader and a C-Level executive from the same company. The executive was going over all the recommendations and demands about an upcoming product launch. He was clearly feeling over-whelmed and looked at the communications leader and said, "I feel like we've swapped roles. If I spend this much time communicating, you'll have to spend some of your time launching the product!" The communications leader was quick to reply, "If you follow this plan, the product will launch itself."

I believe there's a place for an effective and thoughtful communicator somewhere in between. I mentioned in the beginning of Section 3 that executives should have their own personal communication plan. Not only should the plan define messages, but it should also define communication methods. This is an important part of getting your arms around what you can handle.

Here are some of the more important platforms for a current leader and a future leader to consider.

Social Media

For executives, social media can be effective and it can be risky. Within our client base, we see both perspectives. For every executive or senior manager who has launched a successful social voice on Facebook, Twitter, etc., I have seen two who have been burned by it. Curiously, it's the business-to-consumer discussions that have been effective and the business-to-business ones that have not been. But, that's a discussion to have with your communication team.

What I do know is that any communication has to be authentic. I've been asked to ghost write so many blogs and Twitter trails in the last two years that I question how many executives are truly embracing the medium. Social media seems to fall in the category with those who are trying to span it all and send out any word across all platforms.

As I've been told by many audiences, when you consider all the communication pushed out under the name of the CEO, you question whether any of it really comes directly from the C-Suite. Can one human being do it all?

With many clients, we've found that the social media outlets are often a great place to allow another executive or seasoned manager to have a voice.

Video

It doesn't take long for social media to lead to "video media." I've seen many companies leverage great presentations and messages through this tool and it's very effective. We encourage the use of video in remote presentations, webinars, etc. to bring more energy and life to an often flat delivery system.

If video isn't a medium you're comfortable with, you should get there. I believe companies will begin to use it more and more to reach remote audiences. It's a nice transition from live presentations and discussions to at least seeing the executive and feeling a sense of the energy and involvement behind the message.

Video is different than a live audience and it takes practice to deliver this message well. Many executives need to find a way to be authentic and engaging without a live audience. It's possible, but it takes practice to master it.

In recent years, we've been asked to work with executives who struggle with the missing audience. The biggest difference is getting to a point quickly and learning to break content into a series of messages and sound bites. Although video is an integral part of our world today, few of us will sit and watch a corporate video for thirty minutes in the same way we would sit through a live meeting. It's a different format that requires a different approach.

Remote Discussions

Unlike videos which are produced and sent out, remote presentations or discussions are often live. This can also be an unnerving experience. While the audience is there, they aren't nearly as engaged as they would be sitting in the room with you.

Remote delivery works best as a follow-up impression rather than an initial one. I've heard story after story of customer presentations where the senior leader couldn't be there, so they brought him in remotely while everyone else was live in the meeting. It turns out to be disruptive and seldom has the anticipated impact.

The biggest challenge with a remote audience is the attention span. It's hard to hold a group's attention without the 55% of physical attributes that define your presence. Your impressions rely solely on the voice, and it takes a dynamic one to pull this off.

Keep the focus much narrower during a remote discussion than a live presentation and use this vehicle to enhance rather than to replace the more effective and dynamic mediums.

Written vs. Spoken Communication

As I look at all the ways communication has evolved, I'd say that some executives rely more on written methods of communication than spoken methods. That's a trade-off you need to evaluate.

We start many workshops with a discussion of written versus spoken communication. The dynamics of written communication that make it an effective platform center around details, creating a record, and getting a group of people on board with a plan. E-mails, reports, and memos are great for this. In writing, you can lay out a plan and create a record for everyone involved in the plan to follow.

But, you can't motivate them to follow it. That takes spoken communication. If written communication carries detail and content, then spoken communication is the language of contact. Only when we speak to people can we build consensus, establish a connection, and engage a group in a strategy.

Every leader I know will tell you that they didn't establish an executive presence across e-mails or written documents. Written communication may reinforce an impression but it can never outdo or even compete with spoken communication for engagement. For that reason, you need to be sure that your approach to communication methods includes several opportunities to bring a message to life and an audience to action.

Give an Audience What They Want

When we began the intensive interviews to support the survey, I had a number of clients who suggested that I talk to employees and people the senior leaders were trying to engage, not just the leaders themselves. We didn't create a separate survey to do this, but we did host several focus groups to get the perspective of those who are often the target of communication.

Their input was consistent with the power of spoken communication previously mentioned. While written communication is good at detail and direction, employees view it as one-sided. It's pushing information at them rather than trying to share information with them. Worse, they rarely believe it's written by the executive who sends it. Today's audiences are more skeptical and more critical than those twenty years ago. Listeners today want to push back a little and engage in finding solutions. They aren't on board until they are a part of the discussion.

While employees like to hear plain speak from their direct managers and appreciate that opportunity as a place to be honest with their reactions, they believe they deserve face time with the top leaders as well. They like the town halls, open mike meetings, and executive hot seat interactions.

While the communication platforms have expanded and need to be added to your communication strategies, you can't replace or remove the live meetings. It's the closest you'll come to establishing a presence with a group and really being able to motivate and influence others.

You need to be seen as well as heard.

18

Reaching the Younger Generations

A common theme in our discussions with top executives is their concern about connecting with younger generations, especially Millenials. Most executives have young employees and the direction on how to communicate with them is confusing.

Many CEOs say they just don't know this group well. The buzz about the uniqueness of Millennials has added angst for leaders. You can't pick up a human resource magazine these days without an article about managing Millennials, hiring Millennials, or retaining Millennials.

Communication articles are driving leaders to become more socially connected and to go where the Millennials are 24/7. Public relations advisors are pushing leaders to engage with social media and gain visibility. The idea is if you want to reach your young employees, you need to be where they are.

Interestingly, a 2010 study revealed that only 35% of CEOs in large companies are using social media. While communications groups are promoting it, legal advisors discourage it.

CEOs worry about establishing a celebrity image, and, to date, there is little measurable return on the social network investment. The bottom line is that executives aren't as familiar or comfortable with the more relaxed format and chatter that most social networks encourage.

Executives do say that they are sending information out more frequently and more urgently. However, somewhere between all the time and right on time, they are exhausted by the process. Some have said that the amount of their communication has increased by as much as 40% over the last five years.

As a part of our research around executive presence, we talked to groups of young employees to better understand their perspective on internal communication and to define the most effective way to reach them. You may be surprised by what we learned.

First, the Millennials and Generation Xers like attention. They seek feedback and interaction with their immediate managers. They won't wait for bi-annual evaluations; feedback needs to be frequent and immediate. They are more social at work, and it's important to reinforce their desire to interact with each other in relaxed settings as well as business ones. They expect their employer to care about them first as people and then as employees. Most of these needs can be met by their immediate managers and division leaders.

Overwhelmingly, the Millennials prefer to experience their leaders through spoken communication rather than written communication. While they get e-mails, news blasts, and other sound bites, they really want an opportunity to sit down with company leaders and talk.

If you think about it, it makes sense. The Millennials were not raised on the "children should be seen, but not heard" theory. These kids were writing to the president in kindergarten! As one human resource consultant said, they respect authority, but they are not in awe of it. Our informal discussions proved that out. They are eager to see leaders in the "hot seat," to pose tough questions, and to get a sense of a leader's confidence and credibility.

Social media is not as powerful to Millenials as it seems to be to those who are feeling overwhelmed by it. They like being connected to friends, co-workers, and the world, but they realize that it's a one way conversation. More importantly, social media is not how or where they want to connect with the CEO. They don't believe e-mails convey emotion or authenticity. In fact, they don't believe that company leaders write most of the communication that's pushed out to them.

When asked about executive presence, young employees shared the same attributes and values as their senior leaders. The words and descriptions used were consistent with the hierarchy presented in Chapter 3.

One notable difference was their impression of being a leader versus being an executive. Each group of Millennials we spoke to across several different companies responded favorably to the word "leader" and not so favorably to the word "executive." Leaders were defined by their influence more than their position. That validates the idea that Millennials respect those who lead, but are not in awe of position or title.

Here's what some said about presence:

"Presence commands respect. People look up to you for advice, direction, and knowledge when you have presence."

"This is someone I would model myself after…people with presence are true role models."

"Presence comes with an open door policy. Someone with presence makes you feel as if they genuinely care about your ideas and would welcome conversation."

"In order to have a presence, you have to be real and consistent. Too often, our executives appear to be polished. You see them one day and they ask for input and involvement. You ride the elevator with them the next morning and it's as if a different guy showed up."

"You should be a leader before you are named an executive because leaders have followers. Executives just have the big jobs."

So, armed with the validation of presence from young employees, and the knowledge that leaders told us the quantity of their communication has increased, we wanted to know if this communication was effective.

The answer was, not always.

When we explored how executives have increased communication, we found that print messages such as e-mails, tweets, and blogs have multiplied. The more traditional spoken communication methods such as town halls, Q&As, and fireside chats have actually gone down in frequency. That's when our red flag went up. While the employees are pushing for their leaders to get connected, I'm not sure the leaders are actually establishing a connection.

So, what do I tell the CEO who worries about keeping up with the times and being relevant enough for young employees? First and foremost, you have to be authentic and make sure that all employees are getting a sense of who you are and what you're trying to help them accomplish. That's how you'll establish a presence with them.

You should also keep three things in mind:

1. Ask for Perspective: If you haven't asked for feedback on executive communication within your company, you should. Times have changed and you should build your own communication plan (as noted in Chapter 14) to include the Millennials' perspective. They aren't shy; they will tell you what they think!

2. Keep Up Appearances: Communication has become 24/7, and your internal advisors may be telling you to communicate more frequently. It makes sense. But, be sure you're balancing the talking with the listening. Your youngest employees aren't just looking for e-mail blasts; they want an opportunity for you to listen to them. In fact, it doesn't feel like communication to them until they are part of it.

3. Connection is Multi-generational: While our written communication methods and tools have changed significantly over the years, the power of spoken communication and connection has remained a constant. No matter what the age, race, or role of an employee, they all want to see leaders express their beliefs, their strategies, and their convictions. The more consistent you are about doing this, the more all of your employees will come to value the connection.

The truth is that younger employees are consistent and similar about what they want from communication. Like all employees, they desire connection, interaction, and discussion. The difference is the Millennials will be less patient about waiting for it.

For Women Only

Women have surpassed men in graduate degrees and outnumbered them on corporate payrolls. Yet, studies continue to show slow progress in reaching the C-Level. While I don't have the answer to why those opportunities aren't occurring, I do have insights about the challenges women face in establishing an executive presence.

I was initially resistant to working with women's groups. My background has always been on the consulting side of business, and I thought that stereotyping women as communicators was a bad idea. I wasn't sure that women's challenges were unique because my exposure had always been to individuals, and I have found through the years that habits and choices with personal style are universal. I worried that women would think there were different characteristics that define presence for women than those outlined for men.

It took a client scenario to get my attention. Several years ago, I was asked by a large law firm to develop a program for women on effective communication. I said I'd be happy to develop the program but that I wasn't convinced there were communication challenges which were unique to women. The partner leading the effort invited me to a meeting that included five women who worked within the firm.

In this meeting, the partner asked the women to share their experiences of communication in their law practice. While they all came across differently to me, they were consistent in describing their communication challenges such as being ignored in meetings, excluded from discussions, and alienated from others in the firm.

I developed the program and created role-plays to allow the women to explore new choices. The most interesting thing happened. As I observed the exercise, I realized all the women in the room were making the same mistakes. I stopped the exercise and coached them on what I observed. We repeated the exercise and the behaviors were the same. This told me they had unintentional habits that were getting in their way of being successful within the firm.

So, I began talking to women's groups about executive presence, and I paid more attention to the executive women I coached and their stories.

The women who participated in our interviews are very bright and determined. Few of them would say they became leaders on sheer luck and many told us they needed help settling into the leadership environment. Most said they were mentored and coached along the way and I learned that they worked very hard to get where they are.

One thing I have learned through the years is that feedback stops when you get near the top. I talked about this in Chapter 14 and it's truer for women than for men. One out of every two coaching engagements that I begin with a woman includes feedback and input that has been passed along to me, but not shared with her.

The reason for this varies among organizations. Sometimes it's because male leaders just aren't as direct and honest with women or they worry about the reaction to the feedback and don't want to hurt feelings. This is limiting because if they aren't willing to give feedback then they don't have expectations for the behavior or skill to change. And that means the glass ceiling has been reached.

As a coach, I work with women who are rising rapidly through an organization and others who are struggling to get to the next level. Over the years they've shared their challenges with personal style and communication, and I've observed common habits that seem to contribute to their frustrations about getting ahead.

While I still believe styles and habits are unique to the individual, I now believe all women can learn from the impressions and stories below.

Impression #1: I Can Do Everything. Evidence in both our personal and professional lives proves that women can multi-task better than most men. When I work with a woman who is frustrated by her inability to get to the next level, she's often frustrated with her workload as well. Somewhere along the line, women sense that they need to do it all to get ahead.

Contrast that with men who typically learn to do a few things very well rather than trying to do everything. Managers are often unsure of what to do with someone who insists on taking on every task. In fact, it doesn't take long before this good intention can turn into the impression of someone who can't delegate or who doesn't manage others well. Women who try to do everything can get left behind doing all of the little things rather than running the big initiatives.

I have seen this happen more than once. I have worked with a specific company for many years and know most of the key players. One of the most talented women I've met is in a senior client services role. Amy runs all the conferences, special events, and product promotions for the company. I interact with her every year as I support the keynote speakers.

I was part of a discussion about the job opening for Chief Marketing Officer. They were interviewing external candidates and I asked the CEO if anyone internal was up for the job. He told me that Amy had applied and was well qualified, but they just couldn't imagine moving her. No one else knew how to do her job and she made it so easy on all the rest of them. They perceived that it would be too disruptive to move her, and she had unintentionally fostered this impression because she hadn't been working herself out of the role or delegating any of the responsibilities. Amy still insisted on doing every task around these conferences that she had done for years. It was a sad example of someone who got left behind to do all the little things.

Coaching Note: I coach women to hone their skills and excel at something specific, not everything. It's hard to quantify the impact you've had on a department or project if you've done a little of everything. Instead, if you've focused on one project and managed it from start to finish, it's easier to align yourself with success.

––––––––––––

Impression #2: Let's Discuss! Talking is as necessary as breathing for many women and as exhausting as a marathon to many men. Women frequently approach business situations with a desire to talk it through and debate all of the ideas and options, which can translate to, "*She talks too much.*" I'm convinced that women think out loud and men really don't! Women who get bogged down in the details by their desire to talk things out can get alienated by male counterparts.

This scenario played out when I coached a team of three men and one woman for an important new business presentation. These teams are often put together based on the future roles in the new relationship and it can be political to be selected. The four executives were pleased for the recognition and all wanted to be part of securing the new business.

It's always complicated to coach a team and this was no different as we coordinated schedules to work through the content framework. In our first two sessions the woman on the team talked constantly. She had input on every idea and an idea for every topic. The meeting ran over and the men got frustrated. I was able to realign the discussion and complete the framework.

However, one of the men pulled me aside and told me that he planned to talk to the head of sales about removing her from the presentation. He knew the other team members were in agreement. I returned for a follow-up meeting the next week, and she was not there. It became a joke among the three men that time was cut in half and consensus was so much easier without her on the team. Her ideas weren't bad ones, but she talked too much.

Coaching Note: The ability to talk things out is a trait women actually use to their advantage when they are in roles to facilitate or lead discussions. But it's important to learn how to read an audience by listening first. I coach women to listen first and speak last; it isn't always necessary to be heard on every topic. Your presence and non-verbal reactions can say more than your words.

Impression #3: I'm Tough as Nails. Often, women feel as though they have to be aggressive with their communication in the workplace in order to get ahead and be heard. We've always been told, *"Don't let anyone step all over you. Speak up for yourself."* I've experienced that in my career and many clients say they have as well. When a woman is being assertive, at times, it can be perceived as, *"She fights everything."*

Women can seem to put on boxing gloves to defend an idea without realizing they're not in a fight. Men rarely challenge ideas in meetings; they tend to take debates out into the hall. When companies want fighters they promote the football all-star or the Navy Seal. Companies tend to promote women to bring intuitive skills and warmth to a team.

Sadly, there are many aggressive women in the corporate world. They are fighting and they tend to pick other women as their targets. While aggressive behavior does win from time to time, it rarely makes it to the C-Level.

I have worked with many women who were being groomed for a leadership role. One woman is memorable because I watched her rise to the top and fall out of grace over a span of two years. She is very attractive and works hard to get the attention of her male co-workers. She is good at what she does but she often forgets that she's not the only one who is talented. When I first worked with her, I remember how often every discussion focused on what *she* had accomplished and how *she* felt rather than her team. To me, she was a one man band and not likely to succeed at motivating and engaging others. In fact, she told me she really didn't have time for it.

Within the company she made it a point to grab the conversation and belittle others as her visibility continued to rise. Although she started out as a rising star, I saw resistance building in other leaders around her. She was rising in the company but she wasn't gaining respect, support, or camaraderie with her peers. She had the physical qualities of presence but none of the emotional ones.

The CEO had nurtured her advancement, so it took him awhile to realize that she had become ostracized. When she pressed her suggestions on his team, no one asked questions and no one supported her ideas. Her peers had built a team without her and they had no interest in working with her. She was a glitzy executive, but she fell far short of being a leader. She was fired the next year. Hopefully, she learned that the abilities to build relationships and influence others are essential qualities of presence.

Coaching Note: Aggressiveness is not a trait that most people like and it's important for women to understand when they are fighting or pushing others away with their communication style. In many cases, I find that women don't even realize they're being viewed this way. By becoming more aware of these types of impressions, women gain credibility when they simply own who they have become and project a sense of confidence about what they can achieve—all before saying a word.

Management consultants have said for years that women have natural nurturing traits that make them effective as communicators and leaders. I've found that when women are focused on the right qualities and let go of the impressions defined above, they are remarkable leaders.

20
Future Leaders & Succession

The interviews and surveys with senior leaders spanned careers over forty years. While much has changed about business settings and communication tools, their thoughts on executive presence are consistent from their initial observations as young employees to their own experiences as leaders of companies.

This gave them confidence in saying that the demands to present an executive presence to any audience will remain consistent for years to come. Presence truly is:

The confidence to express your ideas with conviction and the ability and desire to engage and influence others in the process.

This brings us back to where our discussion of executive presence began in Chapter 1. Presence is an essential quality for leaders, and organizations have become more proactive and even urgent about developing it in future leaders.

Over the last forty years this has changed. The budget for

high potential training within organizations almost triples that of general training and with good reason. There are skill gaps in the next generation of leaders and these must be closed in order to run the complex organizations of the future.

Presence needs to be part of these programs and used as a benchmark for stretching potential leaders into probable ones. The best approach to incorporating presence in a development program is a combination of three elements:

1. Training: Training provides an opportunity to introduce fundamental skills of presence as highlighted in Chapters 10-12. While each leader exhibits presence differently, basic concepts are common to everyone.

2. Coaching: Coaching gives future leaders an opportunity to adapt skills to their own style. By evaluating feedback and focusing on key situations, they gain confidence and practice in applying the techniques to strengthen impressions.

3. Observing: All future leaders want an opportunity to observe current leaders. Chapter 17 explored many ways to do this, but it takes participation and buy-in from senior management. Not only does interaction with top leaders demonstrate presence, it validates the importance of it.

In many of the development programs we support, the most impactful component is a presentation or report to senior leaders which provides a high profile moment.

Senior level involvement in these programs helps link the company's objective of developing future skills with the participants' objective of getting visibility. While every employee wants to be told they're a high potential candidate, the prospect of leadership feels too far away. In truth, it's a potential, not a promise.

Employees' development objectives are tied to exposure to senior leaders. They believe if you give them exposure to the top executives, they can create their own fast track and their own potential. The balance of both perspectives makes for a successful program.

The executives we interviewed support these programs and are pleased with the impact. But, they added some thoughts about future leaders that are worth considering.

When asked about the rising stars within their own organizations, they said:

"They are brighter than I was twenty years ago."

"They are impatient."

"They don't know as much as they think they do."

"They are super smart and have great intellectual curiosity."

"I can tell a lot about future leaders by the questions they ask me. Some are trying to flatter me and ask questions to get face time. Others ask insightful questions that suggest they're trying to keep up with our company. That tells me that they've invested time outside the room to learn something, and I know I'll see them again."

Today's leaders worry about who is coming up behind them and whether they have the skills to adapt to a multi-cultural workforce. Here's what they said:

"I worry that we put people in bigger roles who don't really understand the world around them."

"Their presence is going to have to transcend cultures. They're going to have to connect communities and diversities within the organization."

"I always look at high performers to see if they have runway ahead of them. It's critical to know that their skills can continue to grow. We've had great people crash and burn because we didn't get them ready for what was ahead of them."

"Patience will be the downfall of the next generation of leaders. They're just too impatient and don't know as much as they think they do."

"They need writing skills. Too many employees can't get their point across."

"Our next leaders will have to demonstrate they don't have the 'it's all about me' mentality."

"They will have to be whip smart. Company cultures are no longer paternal, confrontation will be a regular occurrence. They will have to welcome spirited exchange and then be able to bring closure to it."

"They will have to be transparent. They will have to be honest about what they're doing and how they're doing it in order for people to believe and stay loyal."

"The days of controlling content are over. Future leaders will always be in a two-way dialog."

A two-way dialog is not something to be afraid of but it is

something that requires preparation. Executive presence is the skill and hidden factor leaders use to influence and engage others.

The survey statistics validate the reality of succession. Presence can help you get ahead, but it can also hold you back from a future leadership position. It's a smart quality for a young manager and a career essential for a seasoned one. It is a skill that transcends generations and intensifies as you climb your career ladder.

But, it may always be a little like the emperor with no clothes. Although companies are investing in the awareness and development of presence, it will always be a little elusive because it spans a range of attributes. Every leader has to exhibit physical, functional, rational, and emotional traits. It won't be a single skill that someone gives you, but a variety of skills that you identify, develop, and make your own.

Presence won't be a quick fix but it is an attainable goal. Those who have developed presence have leveraged it to reach the top of companies and create great opportunities.

Here's hoping you make this hidden factor your differentiating one.

Appendix
Survey Results

Survey administered by Fitzgerald+CO
June 4-July 2, 2010

How Important Is Executive Presence In Being A Good Leader?

Respected	91%
Business Knowledge	90%
Strategic Thinker	88%
Executive Presence	80%
People Person	80%
Functional Expertise	75%
Connected/Know the Right People	71%
Risk-Taker	61%

How Do You Define Executive Presence?

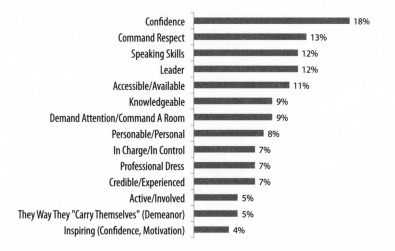

Confidence	18%
Command Respect	13%
Speaking Skills	12%
Leader	12%
Accessible/Available	11%
Knowledgeable	9%
Demand Attention/Command A Room	9%
Personable/Personal	8%
In Charge/In Control	7%
Professional Dress	7%
Credible/Experienced	7%
Active/Involved	5%
They Way They "Carry Themselves" (Demeanor)	5%
Inspiring (Confidence, Motivation)	4%

This was an open-ended question.

Qualities of Executive Presence

Quality	Percentage
Believable	96%
Ability to See the Big Picture	96%
Strong Communicator	95%
Forward-Thinking	95%
Ability to Engage Others	95%
Credibility	95%
Confidence	94%
Ability to Listen to Others	94%
Ability to Influence Others	94%
Professionalism	94%
Drive	93%
Strategic-Thinking	93%
Ability to Persuade Others	93%
Focus	92%
Preparedness	91%
Authentic	91%
Initiative	90%
Ability to Accept Feedback/Criticism	90%
Ability to Collaborate with Others	89%
Ability to Command a Room	88%
Intuitive	88%
Physical Presence (How One Carries Oneself)	88%
Expertise	87%
Ability to Create Excitement	85%
Refinement/Polish	82%
Empathy	82%
Charisma	82%
Global-Thinking	78%
Eagerness	72%
Attire	71%
Transparent	65%
Detail-Focused	59%
Outspoken	52%

Participants ranked a list of qualities.

CEO Self-Evaluation on Qualities of Executive Presence

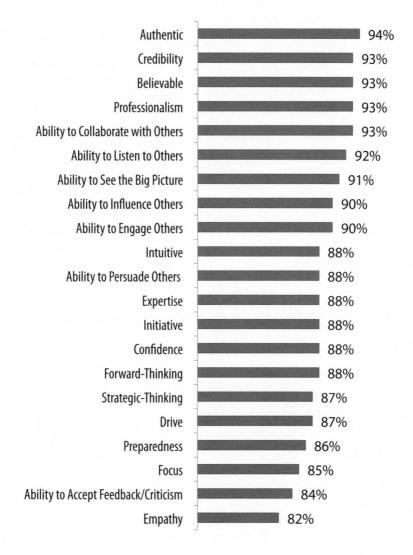

Quality	Percentage
Authentic	94%
Credibility	93%
Believable	93%
Professionalism	93%
Ability to Collaborate with Others	93%
Ability to Listen to Others	92%
Ability to See the Big Picture	91%
Ability to Influence Others	90%
Ability to Engage Others	90%
Intuitive	88%
Ability to Persuade Others	88%
Expertise	88%
Initiative	88%
Confidence	88%
Forward-Thinking	88%
Strategic-Thinking	87%
Drive	87%
Preparedness	86%
Focus	85%
Ability to Accept Feedback/Criticism	84%
Empathy	82%

Importance of Executive Presence at Various Career Levels

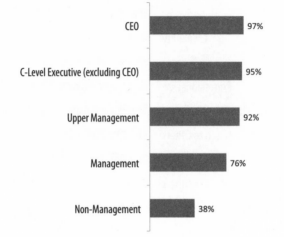

CEO — 97%
C-Level Executive (excluding CEO) — 95%
Upper Management — 92%
Management — 76%
Non-Management — 38%

Identifying Leaders Based on Executive Presence

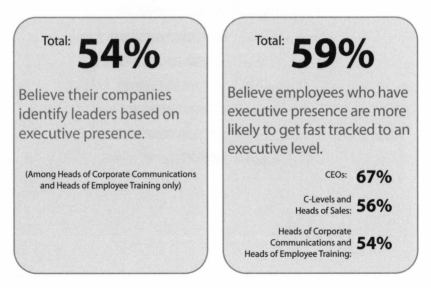

Total: **54%**
Believe their companies identify leaders based on executive presence.

(Among Heads of Corporate Communications and Heads of Employee Training only)

Total: **59%**
Believe employees who have executive presence are more likely to get fast tracked to an executive level.

CEOs: **67%**
C-Levels and Heads of Sales: **56%**
Heads of Corporate Communications and Heads of Employee Training: **54%**

How Executive Presence Is Achieved

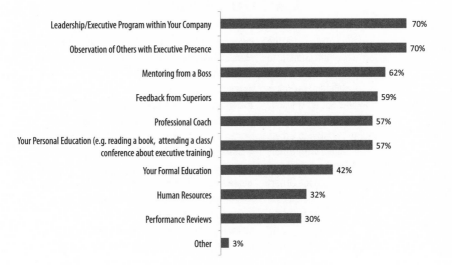

Leadership/Executive Program within Your Company	70%
Observation of Others with Executive Presence	70%
Mentoring from a Boss	62%
Feedback from Superiors	59%
Professional Coach	57%
Your Personal Education (e.g. reading a book, attending a class/conference about executive training)	57%
Your Formal Education	42%
Human Resources	32%
Performance Reviews	30%
Other	3%

Executive Presence & Getting Ahead

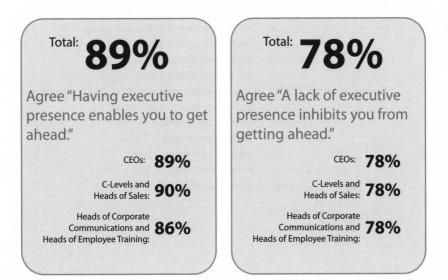

Total: **89%**

Agree "Having executive presence enables you to get ahead."

CEOs: **89%**

C-Levels and Heads of Sales: **90%**

Heads of Corporate Communications and Heads of Employee Training: **86%**

Total: **78%**

Agree "A lack of executive presence inhibits you from getting ahead."

CEOs: **78%**

C-Levels and Heads of Sales: **78%**

Heads of Corporate Communications and Heads of Employee Training: **78%**

Qualities of Executive Presence That Can Be Coached

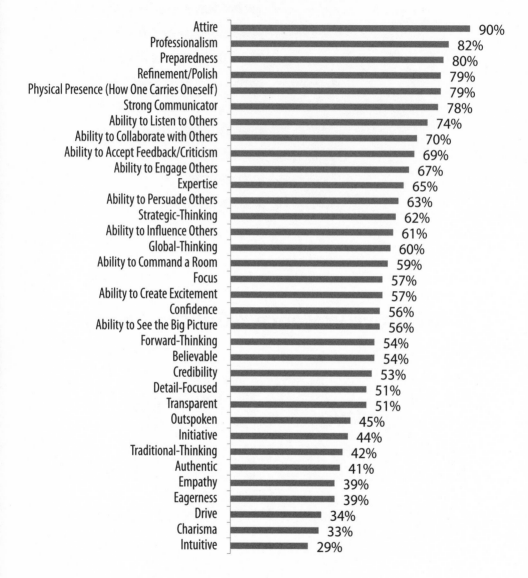

Where You Work the Hardest to Have Executive Presence

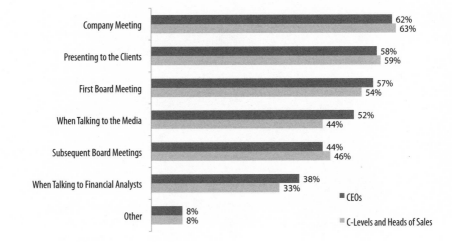

Category	CEOs	C-Levels and Heads of Sales
Company Meeting	62%	63%
Presenting to the Clients	58%	59%
First Board Meeting	57%	54%
When Talking to the Media	52%	44%
Subsequent Board Meetings	44%	46%
When Talking to Financial Analysts	38%	33%
Other	8%	8%

Who Has More Executive Presence?

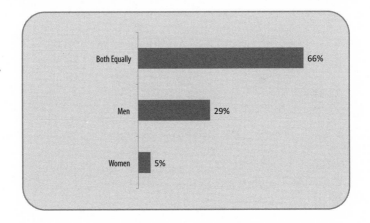

Both Equally	66%
Men	29%
Women	5%

Respondents By Gender

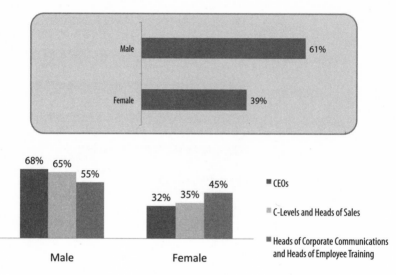

Male	61%
Female	39%

Male
68% 65% 55%

Female
32% 35% 45%

- CEOs
- C-Levels and Heads of Sales
- Heads of Corporate Communications and Heads of Employee Training